Monks and Monasteries: A Brief History

Robert C. Jones

Robert C. Jones
P.O. Box 1775
Kennesaw, GA 30156

robertcjones@mindspring.com

First Edition

ISBN: 1451580002
EAN-13: 9781451580006

This book is dedicated to all the monks and nuns who have toiled without reward for centuries in the name of our Lord.

Table of Contents

Introduction

For 700 years, medieval monasteries in Europe were the spiritual, agricultural, educational, legal, and administrative centers of the areas in which they were located. Following a daily routine of prayer, solitude, and physical labor, the monasteries provided a refuge from the cruel world that was Medieval Europe. In addition, it was the monks (and nuns) of these monasteries who kept alive the spark of knowledge in the West through their patient preservation and hand copying of ancient texts (both Christian and Classical).

This book will discuss the antecedents of the Western monastic movement (both Jewish and Christian), examine its founders and greatest influences (St. Antony, St. Benedict, St. Augustine), examine the great monastic orders in the high Middle Ages (Benedictines, Cluniacs, Cistercians, Franciscans, etc.), and finally, discuss the ebbing of the monastic movement.

Glossary

- **Abbey** – religious community presided over by an abbot or an abbess
- **Abbess** – head of a nunnery (or, occasionally, head of a double monastery – St. Hilda of Whitby)
- **Abbot** – head of an abbey. "In the monastery, he is considered to represent the person of Christ." (*Rule of Benedict* Chapter II)
- **Cenobites** – monks that live in a monastic community, typically under an abbot
- **Dissolution of the Monasteries** – the disbanding destruction of the monasteries in England by King Henry VIII (1536-40)
- **Hermits (or anchorites)** – ascetic solitaries, typically not part of a defined monastic order
- **Lay brother** (especially Cistercian) – member of monastery not required to observe the complete holy office. Often involved in manual labor.
- **Monk** – from Gr. *monos*, man by himself; member of a monastic religious order. Bound to vows of poverty, chastity and obedience. A.K.A. "a religious".

- **Prior** – second in command to an abbot, or head of a priory
- **Priory** – smaller monastic house than an abbey. Often a daughter house of an abbey (all Cluniac houses were priories, except for the one at Cluny). Headed by a *prior*.

Ruins of the abbot's lodgings at Haughmond Abbey, England (Augustinian Canons). The area to the left under renovation was the infirmary. (Photo by Robert C. Jones)

Timeline

Date	Event
1st century	First virgins consecrated to Christ – daughters of Deacon Philip in Acts 21:9
251 A.D.	Early Christian hermit St. Antony is born
3rd century	Clement of Alexandria, Origen, Tertullian, and Cyprian all praise asceticism
320	Pachomius (293-346) founds monastery at Tabennisi in Egypt; later founds nearby nunnery with over 400 nuns
c. 330	St. Amoun and St. Macarius create monasteries in the Egyptian desert
c. 341	Synod at Gangra expresses disapproval of monks that entirely give up church attendance
c. 356	St. Basil (330-379) joins a monastery in Asia Minor; begins work on his *Rules* for monastic living.
386 A.D.	St. Jerome founds monasteries in Bethlehem
4th century	Monasteries begin to appear in the West – St. Ambrose at Milan, St. Hilary at Poitiers, etc.
Late 4th/early 5th century	St. Augustine of Hippo writes several letters and sermons which outline the rules for monastic life
c. 480	Birth of St. Benedict
5th century	• *Laura* organizations appear in Judean desert; several generally solitary monks gathered around one leader – common prayers and meals (similar to later Carthusians) • Symeon the Stylite (c. 390 – 459) lives on top of a column (monastery of Telanissos in Syria) • St. Patrick brings Christianity to Ireland
c. 526	Rule of Benedict written
c. 550	Death of St. Benedict
c. 563	St. Columba founds a monastery at Iona for the purpose of converting Scotland to Christianity
597	St. Augustine, prior of St. Andrew's monastery in Rome, is sent to England as a missionary by Pope Gregory I
c. 663	Synod of Whitby (hosted by St. Hilda) resolves differences between Celtic and Roman Christianity
731	Bede completes *History of the English Church and People*
late 8th-century	Abbeys of northern and eastern England destroyed by Viking raiders (Lindisfarne sacked in 793)
909	Berno founds the monastic house of Cluny
936	Abbot Laffredus of Farfa in Lazio is poisoned by two of his

Date	Event
	monks, for trying to enforce the Benedictine rule
c. 943	St. Dunstan begins monastic reform movement in England
c. 970	English bishops and abbots/abbesses meet with King Edgar to create the *Regularis Concordia*, a constitution for English monasticism. Some practices were peculiar to English monasticism – lay people attending Sunday Mass at the monastic church, for example
1084	St. Bruno founds the Carthusians
1098	Cistercian order founded in Citeaux by Robert Molêsme
1099	First Crusade captures Jerusalem
1115	St. Bernard founds new Cistercian abbey at Clairvaux
1118	Hugh de Payens and eight companions form the Knights Templar in Jerusalem
1127	St. Bernard writes *Apologia* – an indictment of the Cluniacs
1128	Knights Templar adopt Cistercian rule
1170	Birth of St. Dominic in Castile, Spain
1181	Birth of St. Francis of Assisi
1205	St. Dominic begins preaching against the Cather heresy in southern France
1210	Franciscan Order recognized by Pope Innocent III
1217	Pope Honorius III licenses the creation of the "Order of Preachers", later known as the Dominicans
1221	Death of St. Dominic, founder of the Dominican Order
1228	Francis of Assisi canonized
1233	The Dominicans are given the task of running the courts of the Inquisition
1291	Last Christian stronghold in the Holy Lands falls (Acre)
1323	Pope John XXII supports the idea that Christ and the Apostles did not practice absolute poverty – a blow to the stricter Franciscans of the day
1328	Franciscan Spiritual William of Ockham (Ockham's Razor) excommunicated for insisting on strict poverty for monks
1347-51	Bubonic and Pneumonic Plague sweeps through Europe and England; many monasteries devastated
1517	Martin Luther tacks *95 Theses* to the door of Wittenburg Castle, launching the Protestant Reformation
1534	Society of Jesus (Jesuits) formed by Saint Ignatius of Loyola
1536-40	800 religious communities in England and Wales are dissolved by Henry VIII and his secretary Thomas Cromwell
1565	First permanent parish established in America at St. Augustine, Florida
1662	Armand Jean Le Bouthillier de Rancé, abbot of the Cistercian abbey Notre Dame de la Trappe, France, forms the Trappists (Cistercians of the Strict Observance)

Date	Event
1732	Protestant *Seventh Day Baptists* found mixed-gender monastery in Ephrata, Pennsylvania
1769	Junípero Serra founds Mission San Diego de Alcalá at San Diego. Eventually, a total of 21 missions would be established in California (the last in 1823).
1790	Cistercian and Cluniac orders suppressed in France by the French Revolution
1798	Knights of Malta (former Knights Hospitalers) defeated by Napolean I
1830	St. Bernard is declared a doctor of the Church by Pope Pius VIII

Predecessors and Antecedents

The monastic movement which swelled in the West in the 6th and 7th centuries had both Christian and Jewish predecessors.

Nazirites

The Jewish Nazirites, who are mentioned as early as the Pentateuch in the Old Testament, were not a monastic order *per se*, but made it possible for those that wanted to make a "special vow, a vow of separation to the LORD". The Christian monks later echoed these ideas of separation from the normal, and of making a vow to God (Medieval monks vowed poverty, chastity and obedience). The Book of Numbers lists some of the requirements for becoming a Nazirite:

> [2]Speak to the Israelites and say to them: "If a man or woman wants to make a special vow, a vow of separation to the LORD as a Nazirite, [3]he must abstain from wine and other fermented drink...[5]During the entire period of his vow of separation no razor may be used on his head. He must be holy until the period of his separation to the LORD is over; he must let the hair of his head grow long. [6]Throughout the period of his separation to the LORD he must not go near a dead body. [8]Throughout the period of his separation he is consecrated to the LORD." (Numbers 6, NIV)

There appeared to have been two types of Nazirites. The first type (probably a minority) were dedicated at birth:

- Samson (Judges 13:7)
- Samuel (1 Sam 1:11)
- John the Baptist (Luke 1:15)

(The Benedictines would later accept children to be entered into the order for life.)

The second type (probably the most numerous) made their vow for a specified period of time. The most famous is Paul of Tarsus (Acts 18:18).

"Sons of Zadok" and the Essenes

> *Manual of Discipline:* "And this is the order for the men of the community who have offered themselves to turn from all evil and to lay hold of all that he commanded according to his will, to be separated from the congregation of the men of error, to become a community in law and in wealth, answering when asked by the sons of Zadok, the priests who keep the covenant..." (*The Dead Sea Scrolls*, Millar Burrows, p. 376[1])

Among the 800 scrolls found in caves above the Dead Sea settlement of Qumran were 10+ copies of each of two documents that appear to be the rules or "constitution" of a Second Temple Jewish "monastic" order. The documents in question are *The Manual of Discipline* (or the *Rule of the Community*), and the *Damascus Document* (fragments of which were also found in Cairo in 1897). Neither document reveals the name of the community that wrote them, other than the nomenclature "Sons of Zadok".

While one must be careful to not assign attributes of Medieval Christian monasticism to a Jewish religious sect that existed before Christ, there are some remarkable similarities between the rules outlined in the two documents, and the later Christian monastic rules, such as the 6th century *Rule of Benedict*. Some of the rules and attributes of the "Sons of Zadok" which seem to closely parallel the later Christian monastic rules include:

- They were headed by a "superintendent" or "examiner", who seemed to be both teacher and Chief Financial Officer
- Judicial decisions were made by the assembled members of the group
- Apparently there was community ownership of property
- There appears to have been a required two-stage (one year each) probation period for entry into the sect
- At some point they appear to have separated themselves from the rest of Judaism, and settle in a remote area ("When these things come to pass for the community in Israel, by these regulations they shall be separated from the midst of the session of the

---

[1] *The Dead Sea Scrolls*, Millar Burrows, The Viking Press, 1961

men of error to go to the wilderness to prepare there the way of the LORD...”[2]

- Prayer was an important element of their daily worship
- Those that violated Mosaic law and the community rule willfully were excommunicated
- They scrupulously obeyed the Sabbath

So, who were the "Sons of Zadok"? The most common explanation by modern day scholars is that they were Essenes, the mysterious religious group named by 1st century historians Josephus and Pliny the Elder:

> Lying on the west of the [Dead Sea], and sufficiently distant to escape its noxious exhalations, are the Esseni [Essenes], a people that live apart from the world, and marvelous beyond all others throughout the whole earth, for they have no women among them; to sexual desire they are strangers; money they have none; the palm-trees are their only companions. Day after day, however, their numbers are fully recruited by multitudes of strangers that resort to them, driven thither to adopt their usages by the tempests of fortune, and wearied with the miseries of life. Thus it is, that through thousands of ages, incredible to relate, this people eternally prolongs its existence, without a single birth taking place there; so fruitful a source of population to it is that weariness of life which is felt by others. Below this people was formerly the town of Engadda, second only to Hierosolyma in the fertility of its soil and its groves of palm-trees; now, like it, it is another heap of ashes. Next to it we come to Masada, a fortress on a rock, not far from [the Dead Sea]. Thus much concerning Judæa. (*The Natural History*, Pliny the Elder, Translated by John Bostock, M.D., F.R.S., H.T. Riley, Esq., B.A., Ed.[3])

Whether or not the community of the *Manual of Discipline* and the *Damascus Document* were Essenes or not, they do appear to have been a 1st or 2nd-century B.C. Jewish monastic group, whose rules were either later emulated or paralleled by St. Benedict, St. Augustine, and others.

---

[2] *The Dead Sea Scrolls*, Millar Burrows, The Viking Press, 1961
[3] *The Natural History,* London. Taylor and Francis, Red Lion Court, Fleet Street. 1855

The Early Christians

An obvious "early Christian" role-model for later monastic ascetics is to be found in the person of John the Baptist, who preached in the Judean desert, and wore clothes of "camel's hair":

> [1]In those days John the Baptist came, preaching in the Desert of Judea... [4]John's clothes were made of camel's hair, and he had a leather belt around his waist. His food was locusts and wild honey. [5]People went out to him from Jerusalem and all Judea and the whole region of the Jordan. [6]Confessing their sins, they were baptized by him in the Jordan River. (Matthew 3, NIV)

John the Baptist is also one of the several Nazirites mentioned in the Bible that were dedicated at birth to the discipline:

> He is never to take wine or other fermented drink, and he will be filled with the Holy Spirit even from birth. (Luke 1:15, NIV)

Elements that would later be echoed in Western monasticism can also be found in the "primitive" early church as described in Acts. Attributes such as sharing possessions, continual fellowship, teaching and learning, and communal meals were all part of very early Christian practice, as these passages from Acts discuss (see also Acts 4:32-37):

> [42]They continually devoted themselves to the teaching of the apostles, to fellowship, to the breaking of bread, and to prayer. [43]A sense of awe came over everyone, and many wonders and signs were being done by the apostles. [44]All the believers were together, and they shared everything with one another. [45]They made it their practice to sell their possessions and goods and to distribute the proceeds to anyone who was in need. [46]They had a single purpose and went to the Temple every day. They ate at each other's homes and shared their food with glad and humble hearts. [47]They kept praising God and enjoying the good will of all the people. And every day the Lord was adding to them people who were being saved. (Acts 2:42-47, NIV)

There also seems to be some admiration of celibacy and/or singleness in the early church, as these passages from Acts, 1 Corinthians, and 4th-century Bishop Eusebius indicate:

[7]On finishing the voyage from Tyre, we arrived at Ptolemais, greeted the brothers, and stayed with them for one day. [8]The next day we left and came to Caesarea. We went to the home of Philip the evangelist, one of the seven, and stayed with him. [9]He had four unmarried daughters who could prophesy. (Acts 21:7-9, NIV)

[8]Now to the unmarried and the widows I say: It is good for them to stay unmarried, as I am. (1 Corinthians 7:8)

For in Asia also great lights have fallen asleep, which shall rise again on the last day, at the coming of the Lord, when he shall come with glory from heaven and shall seek out all the saints. Among these are Philip, one of the twelve apostles, who sleeps in Hierapolis, and his two aged virgin daughters, and another daughter who lived in the Holy Spirit and now rests at Ephesus... (*The Church History of Eusebius*, Translated By the Rev. Arthur Cushman Mcgiffert, Ph.D., Book 3, Chapter 31[4])

The Desert Monks

> "...he [St. Antony] persuaded many to embrace the solitary life. And thus it happened in the end that cells arose even in the mountains, and the desert was colonized by monks, who came forth from their own people, and enrolled themselves for the citizenship in the heavens." (*Life of St. Antony*, Athanasius, Translated by Philip Schaff, D.D., LL.D. And Henry Wace,D.D.[5])

As early as second century, there were small groups of Christians that renounced marriage and possessions, and lived in remote places. However, Christian monasticism as we know it today probably started in the deserts of Egypt in the late-3rd and 4th centuries. These early monks in Egypt are known as the "desert monks", or "the ascetics".

Some scholars believe that the growth of the desert ascetic movement was in response to the growing cosmopolitan nature of the Church – in c. 312 A.D., the Emperor Constantine converted to Christianity, and eventually made Christianity the official religion of the combined (east and west) Roman empire. Could the Church remain pure while exercising great political and economic power and control?

---

[4] *The Nicene and Post-Nicene Fathers Second Series, Volume 1*, by Philip Schaff, editor

[5] *The Nicene and Post-Nicene Fathers Second Series, Volume 4*, Edited by Philip Schaff, D.D., LL.D.

Some of the desert monks sought to emulate the lives of the Christian martyrs. Others believed that the path to salvation was through constant prayer and supplication to God. This raised a disturbing question that would be raised time and time again throughout the history of monasticism – is a monastic life "dedicated to God" "better" than the lives of normal church-going folks? Better than the non-monastic priests, bishops, and other clerics? And if so, does this mean that there are two "grades" of Christians? Is one more "saved" than the other? Does "subduing natural urges" (one of the goals of the ascetics) attain greater favor in heaven?

One of the earliest of the desert monks is St. Antony (251-356). He is also one of the most famous, by virtue of the *Life of Antony*, written by Athanasius of Alexandria around the time of Antony's death. (Athansius was famous for his anti-Arian writings, as well as his Paschal letter 39, which is the oldest extant listing of the books of the New Testament as we know them today). We will examine St. Antony in some detail, as an example of the desert monk movement.

St. Antony was Egyptian by birth, born into a wealthy family. Upon the death of his parents, Antony renounced his wealth, put a young sister into a convent to be raised, and retired to tombs located outside of his village. Later, he moved into an abandoned fort in a remote mountain area, and resided there for 20 years. Finally, he moved to another area with a spring at the foot of a mountain, where he lived out the rest of his 105 years.

According to the *Life of Antony*, Antony lived a very severe and ascetic life:

> ... he was ever fasting, and he had a garment of hair on the inside, while the outside was skin, which he kept until his end. And he neither bathed his body with water to free himself from filth, nor did he ever wash his feet nor even endure so much as to put them into water, unless compelled by necessity. Nor did any one even see him unclothed, nor his body naked at all, except after his death, when he was buried. (*Life of St. Antony*, by Athanasius, Translated by Philip Schaff, D.D., LL.D. And Henry Wace,D.D.[6])

---

[6] *Ibid*

One of the reasons for the severe life led by Antony was his constant battles with the devil – a recurrent theme throughout his biography:

> But Antony having learned from the Scriptures that the devices of the devil are many, zealously continued the discipline, reckoning that though the devil had not been able to deceive his heart by bodily pleasure, he would endeavor to ensnare him by other means. For the demon loves sin. Wherefore more and more he repressed the body and kept it in subjection, lest haply having conquered on one side, he should be dragged down on the other. He therefore planned to accustom himself to a severer mode of life. (*Life of St. Antony*, Athanasius, Translated by Philip Schaff, D.D., LL.D. And Henry Wace,D.D.[7])

In time, as the fame of Antony spread, cells of monks grew up around Antony's cell, and looked to him for leadership (according to Athanasius, Constantine himself once wrote to St. Antony asking for advice!):

> So their cells were in the mountains, like filled with holy bands of men who sang psalms, loved reading, fasted, prayed, rejoiced in the hope of things to come, labored in alms-giving, and preserved love and harmony one with another...For then there was neither the evil-doer, nor the injured, nor the reproaches of the tax-gatherer: but instead a multitude of ascetics; and the one purpose of them all was to aim at virtue. (*Life of St. Antony*, Athanasius, Translated by Philip Schaff, D.D., LL.D. And Henry Wace,D.D.[8])

Athanasius (who may have had his own agenda) records that Antony was anti-Arian (as was Athanasius), and always bowed down to local ecclesiastical rule (something which not all monks would do in the future – Cluniacs, Knights Templar, etc.) Antony also "worked, however with his hands, having heard, 'he who is idle let him not eat,' and part he spent on bread and part he gave to the needy."[9]

During his long life (105 years), Antony is credited with performing many miracles (including bringing water out of dry land), as well as having the power to heal. This desert monk (with some help from Athanasius) would have a lasting influence on Christian monasticism.

---

[7] *Ibid*
[8] *Ibid*
[9] *Ibid*

("For not from writings, nor from worldly wisdom, nor through any art, was Antony renowned, but solely from his piety towards God."[10]

Antony was not alone in his desert monk-ship. Other monks contemporary with Antony founded monasteries or nunneries in the desert, including St. Pachomius, who in 320 founded a monastery at Tabennisi in Egypt, and Saints Amoun and Macarius in c. 330.

In c. 356, St. Basil (330-379) joined a monastery in Asia Minor, and began work on one of the first "rules" for monastic living (which Benedict credits in *his* famous rule as one of his inspirations).

Several of the post-Nicene Church Fathers either started monasteries, or were monks themselves, including St. Athanasius, St. Augustine of Hippo (North Africa), and St. Jerome (Bethlehem).

---

[10] *Ibid*

The First Western Monastic Movements

Joseph of Arimathea

"Jesus Christ being supported by Joseph of Arimethia as Mary Magdalene gives comfort to the grieving Virgin Mary"[11]

Medieval legend, at least, records that the first monastic settlement in the West was by Joseph of Arimathea in England at Glastonbury, in the first century (37 A.D. or 63 A.D., depending on the source). The basic tenants of this legend (relating to the monastic establishment) go something like this:

- In the year 63 A.D. (or, possibly, earlier) Joseph is sent by the Apostle Philip from Gaul to England, with 11 (or 12, in some accounts) disciples, one of whom is his son Josephes

---

- Joseph lands in the British west country (Somerset), and is granted some land on the Island of Yniswitrin ("Isle of Glass") by a local King, Arviragus
- Joseph and his followers create an ascetic community
- At the bidding of the archangel Gabriel, they build a church of daub and wattle in honor of the Blessed Mary
- After the death of Joseph and his followers, the site is abandoned. Later, the great Benedictine monastery of Glastonbury is built on the site.

The legend is remembered today because it also records that Joseph brought with him (variously) two cruets "filled with blood and sweat of the prophet Jesus", collected when Joseph took Jesus down from the cross, or the Cup from the Last Supper (a.k.a. the Holy Grail, or the Sangreal).

Is there any chance that the legends are true? Tertullian as early as the third century reported that "the haunts of the Britons" were "subjected to Christ". Gildas the Wise (500? - 572? A.D.) reported that the British Isles received the "holy precepts of Christ" in the "latter part of the reign of Tiberius Caesar" (who died in 37 A.D.)

Whether true or no, the monastic settlement ascribed to Joseph of Arimathea didn't last. But other early Western monastic settlements would.

The stark remains of St. Mary's Chapel (1186), said to have been built on the exact spot where Joseph built the first daub and wattle church in 63/64 A.D. (Photo by Robert C. Jones)

St. Benedict and the Rule of Benedict

St. Benedict and his sister, St. Scholastica[12]

Much of Western monasticism as we know it today can fairly be traced to a 6th-century Italian monk named St. Benedict of Nursia (c.

---

[12] Library of Congress LAMB, no. 1517 (A size) [P&P]

480-550). The little that we know about Benedict comes from St. Gregory the Great's *Life of St. Benedict* written around 593-94. According to Gregory, Benedict started his monastic career by living in solitude in a cave at Subiaco, Italy, 30 miles east of Rome, to escape the paganism he saw in Rome. In time, other monks asked him to be their leader, and he eventually started 12 monasteries of 12 monks each in the Subiaco area.

Around 529, Benedict founded the monastery of Monte Cassino, Italy (80 miles S. of Rome). Also around this time, Benedict wrote his famous *Rule* for monastic life. The Rule would be the basis for much of Western monasticism for the next 1000 years, and is still an influence today.

The Rule of Benedict

> "The reason we have written this rule is that, by observing it in monasteries, we can show that we have some degree of virtue and the beginnings of monastic life." (*The Rule of St. Benedict in English*[13])

Many of the precepts of Western monasticism were established in the Rule of Benedict. Some of these are included below:

Precept	From the Rule
"Therefore we intend to establish a school for the Lord's service. In drawing up its regulations, we hope to set down nothing harsh, nothing burdensome."[14] (Prologue)	
12-month novitiate	
Abolition of private property	"Above all, this evil practice must be uprooted and removed from the monastery. We mean that without an order from the abbot, no one may presume to give, receive or retain anything as his own, nothing at all – not a book, writing tablets or stylus – in short, not a single item..."[15] (Chapter 33) see also Acts 4:32

---

[13] *The Rule of St. Benedict in English*, The Order of St. Benedict, The Liturgical Press, 1982

[14] *Ibid*

[15] *Ibid*

Precept	From the Rule
Communal meetings of the abbot and the monks (later to be known as Chapter House)	"As often as anything important is to be done in the monastery, the abbot shall call the whole community together and himself explain what the business is; and after hearing the advice of the brothers, let him ponder it and follow what he judges the wiser course."[16] (Chapter 3)
Communal sleeping arrangements (dormitory style)	"The monks are to sleep in separate beds...If possible, all are to sleep in one place...A lamp must be kept burning in the room until morning."[17] (Chapter 22)
Division of the day into seven offices	Lauds, Prime, Terce, Sext, Nones, Vespers, Compline – "Seven times a day I praise you for your righteous laws." (Psalms 119:164, NIV)
Excommunication in degrees	Rebuking in front of the community, exclusion from table and oratory, shunning, "strokes of the rod", banishment from the community
Humility	Benedict quotes from Luke "Whoever exalts himself shall be humbled, and whoever humbles himself shall be exalted." (Chapter 7)
Importance of manual labor	"Idleness is the enemy of the soul. Therefore, the brothers should have specified periods for manual labor as well as for prayerful reading."[18] (Chapter 48)
Obedience	"They no longer live by their own judgement, giving in to their whims and appetites; rather, they walk according to another's decisions and directions, choosing to live in monasteries and to have an abbot over them."[19] (Chapter 5)

[16] Ibid
[17] Ibid
[18] Ibid
[19] Ibid

Precept	From the Rule
Reading accompanying meals	Church Fathers, Lives of the Saints, Bible
Rule by an abbott	"He is believed to hold the place of Christ in the monastery, since he is addressed by a title of Christ."[20] (Chapter 2)
Self-control	"We must then be on guard against any base desire, because death is stationed near the gateway of pleasure."[21] (Chapter 7)
Silence enforced except at prescribed times (Chapter); Laughter, gossip forbidden	"Monks should diligently cultivate silence at all times..."[22] (Chapter 42)
Some positions within the community are defined in addition to the abbot	**Cellarer** – "...someone who is wise, mature in conduct, temparate, not an excessive eater, not proud, excitable, offensive, dilatory or wasteful..."[23] (Chapter 31) **Prior** - "The prior for his part is to carry out respectfully what his abbot assigns to him, and do nothing contrary to the abbot's wishes or arrangements."[24] **Porter** - "At the door of the monastery, place a sensible old man who knows how to take a message and deliver a reply, and whose age keeps him from roaming about. This porter will need a room near the entrance so that visitors will always find him there to answer them."[25] (Chapter 66)

---

[20] *Ibid*

[21] *Ibid*

[22] *Ibid*

[23] *Ibid*

[24] *Ibid*

[25] *Ibid*

Celtic Monasticism

Celtic Christianity can be traced back to the 5th century with the evangelizing efforts of St. Patrick (389 - 461). Patrick was probably born in Scotland, and was captured by Irish pirates when he was 16 years old. He tended flocks in Ulster for several years as a slave, but eventually escaped. He went to France and became a monk, and returned to Ireland in 432 as a missionary. St. Patrick is said to have founded 300 churches and baptized 120,000 people in Ireland in his lifetime.[26] Legend says that St. Patrick also visited Western Britain in 433, and served as an early abbot of Glastonbury Abbey.

St. Patrick[27]

By the 6th century (not long after the death of St. Patrick), a vibrant form of monasticism was being established in Western Britain and Ireland – Celtic monasticism. Celtic monasticism was more ascetic and disciplined than Roman monasticism, and tended to have less

---

[26] World Book Encyclopedia, Field Enterprises Educational Corporation, 1963
[27] Library of Congress LC-USZ62-31937

emphasis on the monastic community (monks often lived in individual cells).

Celtic monasticism was also avidly evangelistic, sending out missionaries to Scotland, Northumbria, and parts of Europe. One of the most famous missionary journeys was that of St. Columba (c. 521-597), who established a monastery on the island of Iona, for the purpose of converting the Picts (Scotland). St. Columban (c. 543 – 615) led a missionary journey to Europe, and founded monasteries in France and Italy (!) Another famous missionary was Aidan, who founded a monastery at Lindisfarne in Northumbria, for the purpose of converting Northern England.

Celtic monasticism was also known for it's emphasis on learning, and on preserving the great works of the past. The most famous book of Celtic monasticism is the intricately illuminated *Book of Kells*, a copy of the Gospels dating to the 8th or 9th century.

Celtic monasticism didn't follow the *Rule of Benedict*, nor did they view themselves as beholden to Rome. Over time, they developed several practices that were different enough from Roman monasticism to attract the attention of Rome. These differences included maintaining a different calendar than Rome (celebrating Easter on a different day), and wearing a different tonsure (shaving of all of the top of the head).

In 663, a great Synod was held at Whitby, under the patronage of Hilda of Whitby (614-680). The Synod of Whitby (King Oswy making the final decision) decided against the Celtic calendar and tonsure, ensuring that Celtic monasticism in the future would have a more Roman flavor.

Celtic monasticism might have become the predominant form of monasticism in Britain, had not Pope Gregory sent St. Augustine in 597 A.D. to bring Britain into the Roman fold. Augustine founded several monasteries, and served as the first Archbishop of Canterbury.

Remains of 11th century Benedictine Monastery Whitby Abbey. In 663, Whitby was the site of the Synod of Whitby, which decided in favor of Roman, rather than Celtic, monasticism. (Photo by Robert C. Jones)

The Great Medieval Orders

The zenith of Western monasticism was from the period starting with St. Benedict in the 6th century, lasting until about the 13th century. But even during that period of ascendancy, Western monasticism still faced varying cycles of decline and reform. As a matter of fact, as we discuss some of the major medieval orders in this next section, many of them were created to combat perceived laxity on the part of their antecedents.

The medieval monastic orders were also interesting studies in economics. It seems that putting a bunch of zealous men that work for free in a rigidly controlled and disciplined environment can lead to great profits for the controlling authority – the monastery or the Order. A good example is the Cistercians, who became the leading wool merchants of their day, or the almost unimaginably wealthy Knights Templar. In both cases, the profligate wealth eventually led to their downfall.

Benedictines

The first and most influential of the great Medieval orders were the Benedictines, sometimes called the "Black Monks", after the color of their robes. This is the monastic order which grew out of the *Rule of Benedict* in the 6th century. Many of the great monasteries of the Middle Ages were Benedictine, such as Glastonbury, Canterbury, and Whitby.

Their influence can not be underestimated. Fifty Popes (including Pope Gregory the Great, father of Gregorian Chant) have come from the Benedictine order. There were approximately 37,000 Benedictines at the beginning of the 14th century.

During the Middle Ages, the abbot of a powerful Benedictine monastery often served as the local landlord, judge, and – in England –Parliamentarian. The abbot, of course, also presided over his monks with almost total authority.

Over time, Benedictine monasteries developed many positions of authority that were not defined in St. Benedict's original rule. The people that filled these positions were known as obedientiaries, and included (among others):

- **Precentor** – in charge of copying manuscripts
- **Sacrist** – running of the Abbey church
- **Chamberlain** – monks sleeping quarters, clothing, bathing
- **Kitchener and refectorer** – in charge of food and drink
- **Almoner** – in charge of alms for the poor
- **Infirmarian** – head of infirmary or hospital
- **Master of works** (sometimes the **sacrist**) – in charge of new building

The former Benedictine Priory at Binham (Norfolk), founded around 1091 as a dependency of St. Albans (Photo by Robert C. Jones)

The Benedictine order included nuns as well as monks (although mixed houses like Whitby were rare). It is said that St. Benedict and his sister St. Scholastica founded the first order of Benedictine nuns.

The Benedictines experienced a steady decline in the number of monks after the 14th century, culminating with a mere 5,000 during the century of the Reformation – helped along by Henry VIII's Dissolution of the Monasteries in 1536-40. However, the order is far from dead today – it has at least 30 monasteries in the United States alone.

St. Dunstan and Glastonbury Abbey

The origins of Glastonbury abbey are shrouded in legend. As discussed earlier in this book, legend has it that Joseph of Arimathea brought the Holy Grail (or two cruets of the blood of Christ) here in 63 A.D. (or 37 A.D. depending on which branch of the legend one wishes to follow). Joseph created a small monastic settlement (perhaps the first in the West), with 11 (or 12) followers.

Whether the legend of Joseph is true of not, the site lay abandoned for many years after the death of Joseph and his followers.

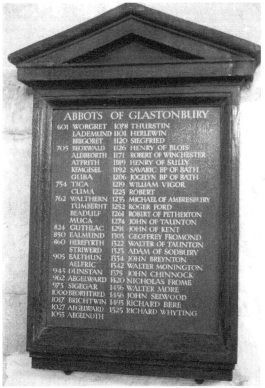

"Abbots of Glastonbury" (Photo by Robert Jones)

Legend says that St. Patrick was the abbot of Glastonbury in the mid part of the 5th century, but it is difficult to prove or disprove this theory. As can be seen in the photo above, the "official" establishment of Glastonbury Abbey was in 601, with one Worgret as the first abbot.

The first famous abbot of Glastonbury was Dunstan, who became abbott in 943. St. Dunstan (c. 925–988) spearheaded the monastic reform movement in Britain in the 10th century. Dunstan was actually born near Glastonbury, and his mother received what she thought was a heavenly sign that her unborn sun would be the "minister of eternal light" to the Church in England.

As a child, Dunstan received his education in Glastonbury Abbey, which had fallen on hard times in the early 10th century. He served in the "old church" at Glastonbury, built on the site of Joseph of Arimathea's church from the 1st century A.D. In time, he became a monk, and lived in a small hermitage located on the Abbey grounds. In 943, Dunstan was personally appointed abbot of Glastonbury by King Eadmund. At this time (if not before), Glastonbury became a Benedictine house, and followed *The Rule of Benedict*. From Dunstan's reign as abbot onward, Glastonbury became one of the richest and most influential monasteries in the world.

Sometime around 957, Dunstan was appointed bishop of first Worcester, and then London. In 960, he was made Archbishop of Canterbury. Sixteen years of peace, prosperity, and monastic growth followed. He died in 988, and was canonized in 1029 (remarkably quickly, by modern standards).

The end of the 12th century saw a rapid succession of key events. A great fire occurred in 1184, destroying the church which had been built over the site of the original church of Joseph of Arimathea. In 1186, a new church, St. Mary's Chapel, was consecrated on the same site. Also in that year, construction on what would become the largest church (565 feet) in England began.

Ruins of the monastic church at Glastonbury (Photo by Robert C. Jones)

In 1191, an event took place that put Glastonbury Abbey "on the map", so to speak. Acting on a tip from King Henry II of England, the monks of Glastonbury reportedly dug up the bones of King Arthur and his wife in an ancient cemetery located near St. Mary's Chapel (St. Joseph's Chapel). An iron cross with the inscription "HERE IN THE ISLE OF AVALON LIES BURIED THE RENOWNED KING ARTHUR, WITH GUINEVERE, HIS SECOND WIFE" was said to have been found above the hollowed out oak coffin. The discovery of the grave caused a sensation in England, and made Glastonbury a popular destination for religious pilgrims until the Dissolution. In 1278, Arthur's bones were interred by King Edward I in a tomb located near the high altar of Glastonbury Abbey.

The legend of the founding of Glastonbury by Joseph of Arimithea served the abbey well in the high Middle Ages. Not only could England claim to be the first Christianized Western country, it was founded by a disciple of Christ himself! And if the 37 A.D. date of founding was correct (as opposed to the more popular 63 A.D.), then the church in England was founded before the church in Rome (!) The claim of Glastonbury's early foundation was advanced at four church councils: the Council of Pisa (1409), Constance (1417), Sienna (1424) and Basle (1434).[28] Glastonbury was known as "Roma Secunda" in some circles during the Middle Ages.

Glastonbury Abbey was formally dissolved by Henry VIII in 1539 (one of the last of the great houses to be dissolved). Abbot Richard Whiting, the last abbot (1525–1539), was unceremoniously hung by order of Thomas Cromwell on the Glastonbury Tor on November 15, 1539, on the spurious charge of "robbery".

The Glastonbury Tor (with St. Michael's Chapel at the peak) (Photo by Robert C. Jones)

In 1965, Queen Elizabeth II erected a wooden cross at Glastonbury with the following inscription:

> The cross. The symbol of our faith. The gift of Queen Elizabeth II marks a Christian sanctuary so ancient that only legend can record its origin.

---

[28] *Glastonbury Abbey: The Holy House at the Head of the Moors Adventurous*, By James P. Carley, The Boydell Press, 1988

The Glastonbury cross (Photo by Robert C. Jones)

The Cluniacs

The Cluniacs were founded at Cluny in France in 910 A.D. by William the Pious, Duke of Aquitaine. Like the later Knights Templar, the Clunaics were placed under direct jurisdiction of the Pope. As such, there was no local episcopal control of the order.

The Cluniacs were known for their great focus on liturgy and meditation on scripture, as well as ornate churches. And while they ostensibly strictly followed the Rule of Benedict, they did not include manual work as part of a monk's daily routine. This was in stark contrast to the Rule of Benedict, which stressed the importance of manual labor.

Unlike the Benedictines, where local abbots had significant authority, all Cluniac houses were ruled from the abbey at Cluny, and all daughter houses were considered priories — a sort of monastic feudal system.[29] Also unlike the Benedictines, the Cluniacs tended to recruit from the nobility. Many of the monks were also priests.

The Cluniacs were spectacularly successfully for the first 200 years of their existence - within 200 years of their founding, they had established over 2000 houses! As was the case with most medieval mon-

---

[29] In fact, monks had to travel to Cluny in order to join the order

astic orders, the Cluniacs became very prosperous in time, which tended to blur the initial ascetic zeal that existed at the foundation. Also, their excess of ritual may have helped lead to their eventual downfall. In the 12th century, for example, St. Bernard of Clairvaux spoke out strongly against the order. By the end of the 12th century, the Cluniacs were already in decline.

Ruins of Castle Acre Priory, Norfolk, England – an 11th-century Cluniac house (Photo by Robert C. Jones)

Carthusians

One religious order that has never needed reforming in its history is the Carthusians, which still exists as an order today. St. Bruno founded the Carthusians (*The Poor Brothers of God of the Charterhouse*) as an ascetic order in 1084, probably in reaction to the excessive riches of the Cluniacs. The order, founded in Grande Chartreuse, France (near Grenoble) stressed poverty, penance, silence, and manual work.

Rather than basing their order on the *Rule of Benedict*, the Carthusians used the more ascetic desert monks as their role models. Unlike most monastic communities, the Carthusian monks lived in individual cells, and only met communally for vespers and matins (and for feast days, funerals, etc.) Carthusian monks fasted often, never ate meat and rarely drank wine. During Lent, they flagellated themselves once a day (!)

Interestingly enough, the Carthusians were introduced in England (1178) by Henry II as part of his penance for the death of Saint Thomas Becket. In England, the *Chartreuse* Houses were referred to as "Charter Houses".

Mount Grace Priory, in North Yorkshire, was a Carthusian monastery, founded in 1398 (Photo by Robert C. Jones)

Bernard of Clairvaux & the Cistercians

> "St. Bernard was a man of lofty mind, whom I almost venture to set above all other celebrated teachers both ancient and modern..." (*To the Councilmen of All Cities in Germany*, Martin Luther, 1524[30])

Perhaps the greatest of the monastic reform movements of the Middle Ages involved the Cistercians, led by (although not founded by) St. Bernard of Clairvaux (1090–1153) the most influential church-man of the 12th century. The Cistercians were founded in 1098 in Citeaux (*Cistercium* in Latin), France (Burgundy), by Saint Robert of Molesme.

---

[30] Ages Software, 1998

The Cistersians were founded on the ideal of returning to a strict interpretation of the *Rule of Benedict*, which the Cistercian leaders felt had been neglected by both Benedictines and Cluniacs. The order grew rapidly in both numbers and influence – within 200 years, they had over 740 communities.

The Cistercians were known as the "White Monks", because they wore a habit of unbleached cloth. To better remove themselves from the secular world, they settled far from towns, often reclaiming inhospitable land in very remote places (Fountains, Rievaulx and Tintern Abbeys in Britain/Wales are all good examples). The monks were dedicated to three activities - worship, study and work.

One important feature of life in a Cistercian monastery was the *lay brothers*, those attracted to the monastic life, but not wishing to live the strict life of a monk. The lay brothers typically tended to the agricultural and livestock needs of the Abbey, often living at remote *granges* – a farmstead within a day's ride of the abbey. In some abbeys, the lay brothers outnumbered the monks by a 4-1 margin, such as at Rievaulx Abbey under Abbot Ailred, which had 150 monks and 600 lay-brothers.

An example of an abbey barn, located near Glastonbury, England (Photo by Robert C. Jones)

The most famous Cistercian was Bernard of Clairvaux. Bernard became a Cistercian in 1112, and in c. 1115, he founded a new Cistercian Abbey at Clairvaux, which had over 700 monks at its height. By the time of Bernard's death in 1153, Clairvaux had spawned 68 daughter houses.

Bernard was outspoken in his criticism of the ornate churches of the Cluniacs. He wrote a scathing indictment of the Cluniacs in 1127, called the *Apologia*, in which he said (of the Cluniacs):

> What is the object of all this?...the church walls are resplendent, but the poor are absent...what has all this imagery to do with monks? What with those who profess poverty and spirituality of mind? (St. Bernard[31])

Under St. Bernard, rules were drawn up which forbade paintings, sculptures, precious metals etc. in Cistercian churches. As a result, Cistercian monasteries are among the least ornate of any monastic houses.

Bernard, like St. Antony 900 years before, was said to have the power of healing. He is also remembered for being an avid advocate of the Crusades. He not only secured official recognition of the Knights Templar (Synod of Troyes, 1128), he is said to have almost single-handedly ordered the Second Crusade (1146). In 1830, St. Bernard was declared a doctor of the Church by Pope Pius VIII.

Organizationally, the Cistercians were somewhere in the middle between the decentralized Benedictines, and the "command and control" Cluniacs. Every year, abbots were expected to return to the grand chapter of the order in Citeaux. By definition, the abbot of Citeaux was head of order. However, daughter house abbots could inspect Citeaux. Steven Harding, an Englishman who was Abbot of Citeaux from 1110–1134, drew up the constitution of the Cistercians (*Carta Charitatis*, the Rule of Love) in 1119. The Cistercians had fewer monks with special titles than the Benedictines – the cellarer was the principle officer next to the abbot.

---

[31] Reprinted in *Life in Medieval Times*, Marjorie Rowling, Perigee Books, 1968

Over time, the Cistercian abbeys in England became big producers of wool, which was sold overseas to weavers in Flanders and Florence. As such, the order became very rich.

In 1664, a reform group known as Trappists arose within the Cistercians, led by Abbot de Rancé (1626 - 1700) in the Abbey of La Trappe, France. As was the case with so many other monastic reform movements, the focus of this reform was to return Cistercians to a stricter observance of their Rule (*The Rule of Benedict*, in this case). Today, the Trappists are known as the Cistercian Order of the Strict Observance. According to the OCSO Web site, there are 100 Trappist monasteries, and 69 nunneries in the world today, and:

> There are now slightly more than 2500 Trappist monks and 1800 Trappistine nuns worldwide, which makes an average of 25 members in each community, less than half as many as in former times.[32]

Trappist Monastery of the Holy Spirit in Conyers, Georgia, founded in 1944 (Photo by Robert C. Jones)

The Cistercians were suppressed in England by Henry VIII, and in France by the French Revolution.

---

[32] http://www.ocso.org/HTM/net/faq-eng.htm

Tintern, a Cistercian monastery located in Wales, was founded in 1131 and dissolved in 1536 (Photo by Robert C. Jones)

The Canons

A slight variation on the medieval model of monasticism was created by the Augustinian and Premonstatensian canons of the 11th and 12th century. The Augustinian (or Austin) Canons were founded in 1059, while the Premonstatensians Canons were found a century later in 1120 (receiving papal sanction in 1126), in Premontre, France. Both groups of canons followed the *Rule of St. Augustine*, which was based on writings of St. Augustine of Hippo.

Both orders lived in communities, but were much more likely to journey out and serve the people in the local communities as priests, manning hospitals, and the like. Most Augustinian houses were under the control of the local bishops.

Ruins of the early 12th century Augustinian Guisborough Priory (Photo by Robert C. Jones)

The 16th century Augustinian Monastery of Acolman, located near Teotihuacan in Mexico (Photo by Robert C. Jones)

The Rule of Augustine

Augustine never wrote a rule for monastic living, in the sense that St. Benedict did. However, in a letter to the nuns at Hippo (423), he outlined some basic precepts of monastic living. This letter, along with parts of other writings of St. Augustine would be adapted into a rule during the Middle Ages. Some excerpts from this letter follow.

The rules which we lay down to be observed by you as persons settled in a monastery are these: —

First of all, in order to fulfill the end for which you have been gathered into one community, dwell in the house with oneness of spirit, and let your hearts and minds be one in God. Also call not anything the property of any one, but let all things be common property, and let distribution of food and raiment be made to each of you by the prioress, — not equally to all, because you are not all equally strong, but to every one according to her need. For you read in the Acts of the Apostles: "They had all things common: and distribution was made to every man according as he had need." Let those who had any worldly goods when they entered the monastery cheerfully desire that these become common property. Let those who had no worldly goods not ask within the monastery for luxuries which they could not have while they were outside of its walls...

Let them, moreover, not hold their heads high because they are associated on terms of equality with persons whom they durst not have approached in the outer world; but let them rather lift their hearts on high, and not seek after earthly possessions, lest, if the rich be made lowly but the poor puffed up with vanity in our monasteries, these institutions become useful only to the rich, and hurtful to the poor. On the other hand, however, let not those who seemed to hold some position in the world regard with contempt their sisters, who in coming into this sacred fellowship have left a condition of poverty...

Be regular in prayers at the appointed hours and times...

Keep the flesh under by fastings and by abstinence from meat and drink, so far as health allows...

If those who are weak in consequence of their early training are treated somewhat differently in regard to food, this ought not to be vexatious or seem unjust to others whom a different training has made more robust...

Let your apparel be in no wise conspicuous; and aspire to please others by your behavior rather than by your attire...

Though a passing glance be directed towards any man, let your eyes look fixedly at none; for when you are walking you are not forbidden to see men, but you must neither let your desires go out to them, nor wish to be the objects of desire on their part...

Keep your clothes in one place, under the care of one or two, or as many as may be required to shake them so as to keep them from being injured by moths; and as your food is supplied from one storeroom, let your clothes be provided from one wardrobe...Therefore the more fully that you give to the common good a preference above your personal and private interests, the more fully will you be sensible of progress in securing that, in regard to all those things which supply wants destined soon to pass away, the charity which abides may hold a conspicuous and influential place....

Let your clothes be washed, whether by yourselves or by washerwomen, at such intervals as are approved by the prioress, lest the indulgence of undue solicitude about spotless raiment produce inward stains upon your souls. Let the washing of the body and the use of baths be not constant, but at the usual interval assigned to it, i.e. once in a month...

Quarrels should be unknown among you, or at least, if they arise, they should as quickly as possible be ended, lest anger grow into hatred, and convert "a mote into a beam," and make the soul chargeable with murder...

Obey the prioress as a mother, giving her all due honor, that God may not be offended by your forgetting what you owe to her: still more is it incumbent on you to obey the presbyter who has charge of you all...

The Lord grant that you may yield loving submission to all these rules, as persons enamored of spiritual beauty, and diffusing a sweet savor of Christ by means of a good conversation, not as bondwomen under the law, but as established in freedom under grace. That you may, however, examine yourselves by this treatise as by a mirror, and may not through forgetfulness neglect anything, let it be read over by you once a week... (*Letter 211*, A.D. 423, St. Augustine, Translated by the Rev. J. G. Cunningham, M.A.[33])

---

[33] *The Nicene and Post-Nicene Fathers First Series, Volume 1*, by Philip Schaff, editor

St. Augustine[34]

The Military Orders - Knights Templar, Knights Hospitalers

The successful crusades of the late 11th/early 12th centuries spawned a curious new kind of monk – the warrior monk. Could monks dedicated to God also be fighting men? Two important groups, the Knight Templars and the Knights Hospitallers were exactly that.

The Knights Templar were founded in 1119 A.D. to protect pilgrim routes to the Holy Lands. They operated out of what they believed were the ruins of the Temple of Solomon in Jerusalem (hence the name, Knights Templar). The Templars received the backing of St. Bernard of Clairvaux (who may have been involved in their founding), and they became nominal Cistercians (1128). Over time, these warrior monks became key figures in the Crusades (one source estimates that over 20,000 Knights Templar were killed in the Crusades). The Templars were notable for the fact that they answered only to the Pope, and not to any local ecclesiastical authority.

In time, the Templars established local offices (called Temples) throughout Western Christendom. Always innovative, they started what is considered by many to be the first European banking system,

[34] Library of Congress LAMB, no. 891 (AA size) [P&P]

and it was their involvement as bankers that eventually led to their downfall. By the early 1300s, King Philip IV of France was deeply in debt to the Paris Temple. In 1307, he charged the order with heresy. Charges eventually brought against the Templars included that postulants were required to deny Christ and spit on the cross, and that the Templars worshiped a mysterious head named "Baphomet" (perhaps a mangling of "Mohammed"?) These charges were never proved, except in confessions received under torture at the hands of the Inquisition.

The Council of Vienne in 1312 officially dissolved the order, giving much of their property to a similar order, named the Hospitalers (see below). The final part of the saga of the Knights Templar occurred in 1314, when Templar Grand Master Jacques de Molay was burned alive, after recanting of an earlier confession.

After the Templars were dissolved, the French crown received cancellation of all debts owed to the Templars, as well as much of their monetary wealth. At their peak in the 13th century, it is estimated that the Templars owned 9000 castles and manor houses.

A similar group of warrior monks were formed in c. 1110, originally to man hospitals in the Holy Lands – *The Knights of the Order of the Hospital of St. John of Jerusalem*, or the *Knights Hospitalers*. Like the aforementioned canons, the Hospitalers operated under the *Rule of St. Augustine*. The Hospitalers started out in Jerusalem, then moved to Acre (1187), Cyprus (1291), Rhodes (1310) and finally Malta (1530). They were forced out of Malta in 1798 by Napolean I, but still exist today as the *Knights of Malta*.

The Rise of Friars – Dominicans & Franciscans

> "Neither the rule of Augustine, nor of Benedict, nor of Bernard." - St. Francis of Assisi

The last great monastic movement of the Middle Ages was that of the mendicant friars – monks dedicated to a life of poverty, and often existing only on handouts as they roamed around the countryside. Two orders of friars are particularly notable, although they couldn't be more different – the Dominicans and the Franciscans.

The founder of the Domincans, St Dominic, was born Domingo de Guzman at Calaruega, Castile, in 1170. He eventually became an Augustinian canon (see above), and adopted a life of poverty. Dominic devoted most of the latter part of his life (beginning in 1205) preaching against and trying to convert the "heretic" Cathars in the Languedoc area of France.

In 1217, Pope Honorius III, impressed by the efforts of Dominic to convert heretics through his zealous preaching, licensed the creation of the "Order of Preachers", also known as the Black Friars (because they wore white robes with black capes), and the "dogs of the Lord" (*Domini canes*). Later, they would be known primarily as Dominicans. At the time of Dominic's death in 1221, there were 60 Dominican monasteries. By 1237, there were over 300.

In 1233, the Dominicans were given the task of running the courts of the Inquisition, a task which they took to with great ferocity and effectiveness for the next several hundred years.

Famous Dominicans of the Middle Ages included St. Thomas Aquinas, St. Catherine of Sienna, St. Peter Martyr, and Torquemada, the Grand Inquisitor of Spain in the time of Columbus.

St. Francis statue at Mission Santa Clara, California (Photo by Robert C. Jones)

The second group of mendicant friars that arose during the 13th century was the Franciscans. The Franciscans were founded by St. Francis of Assisi (1181 – 1226), the son of a wealthy merchant. In 1206, Francis gave up his wealth and embraced a life of poverty and service to the poor. He founded the Franciscan order in 1209-10. (The Order was officially sanctioned by Pope Innocent III in 1210, after Francis wallowed in the mud with some pigs to prove his humility to the Pope!)

During the Fifth Crusade, St. Francis crossed enemy lines in Egypt to preach to the Moslem sultan. The preaching was not successful, but the sultan returned Francis safely to Crusader lines.

The Franciscans originally had no formal monastic houses, and lived a life of absolute poverty – taking their cue from the Biblical injunctions in Matthew 6, such as:

²⁸And why do you worry about clothes? See how the lilies of the field grow. They do not labor or spin. ²⁹Yet I tell you that not even Solomon in all his splendor was dressed like one of these. ³⁰If that is how God clothes the grass of the field, which is here today and tomorrow is thrown into the fire, will he not much more clothe you, O you of little faith? ³¹So do not worry, saying, "What shall we eat?" or "What shall we drink?" or "What shall we wear?" ³²For the pagans run after all these things, and your heavenly Father knows that you need them. ³³But seek first his kingdom and his righteousness, and all these things will be given to you as well. ³⁴Therefore do not worry about tomorrow, for tomorrow will worry about itself. Each day has enough trouble of its own. (Matthew 6:28-34, NIV)

In time, after the death of Francis, the order did start to have buildings to call their own. One group of Franciscans, known as the Spirituals, wished to maintain the ideal of absolute poverty originally promulgated by their founder. They ran afoul of the Inquisition, and were harshly suppressed – it seems that they expected all church officials, including Rome, to live in complete poverty!

Famous medieval Franciscans included Duns Scotus, William of Ockham, Dante, Ubertino of Casale, Father Junípero Serra and Roger Bacon.

There were many similarities between the Domincans and the Francsicans – even though there was great rivalry between the two orders in the Middle Ages. Both were primarily devoted to the laity – healing the sick, "saving" the heretics, acting as missionaries. Both orders served as Inquisitors, during the darkest days of the Inquisition. Both orders were dedicated to the ideal of monastic poverty. And both Orders answered only to the Pope. Perhaps the main difference between the two was the great emphasis that the Dominicans put on the study of logic and theology – the better to combat the arguments of heretics! St. Francis, on the other hand, put little emphasis on "book learning".

Jesuits

By the 1540s, the Roman Catholic Church was reeling from the affects of Protestantism all through Europe. While once the pope reigned supreme over all of Western Christendom, by 1540, whole countries had been lost to Protestant usurpers, including England (Henry VIII), Germany (Luther) and Switzerland (Calvin). France, too, was starting to look shaky, as a growing community of Calvinists (Huguenots) were asserting their rights there. And (unthinkably!) Protestantism was even making inroads into Italy itself! The Roman Church viewed that something must be done to stem the tide of defections. The set of methodologies employed to do so is collectively known as the Counter Reformation.

The Counter Reformation used several methods to attempt to save the church. One was to call a great church council - the Council of Trent met from 1545–1563, and enacted many church reforms, and restated basic Catholic beliefs. Other methods included reconstituting the Papal Inquisition, and open warfare against Protestant strongholds (The 30 Years War, in Germany). Finally, the creation of a new militant religious order, the Jesuits, came out of the Counter Reformation.

The Jesuits, or The Society of Jesus, were founded by Saint Ignatius Loyola and six compatriots in Paris in 1534. (They were officially recognized by the Pope in 1540). Like almost all monks, they take vows of poverty, chastity and obedience, as well as a special vow to the Pope ("I further promise a special obedience to the Sovereign Pontiff in regard to the missions according to the same apostolic letters and Constitutions"). However, unlike many religious orders, their world didn't revolve around the monastery.

The Jesuits were created to defend the Church from attack, and they became a key bulwark against the spread of Protestantism. In time, Jesuits also became famous for missionary work (especially to China), education, and logical thinking.

By 1773, the Jesuits had become so powerful, that there were calls for their suppression (similar to the Knights Templar in the 14th century). The Pope officially suppressed the order except in Russia. The ban stayed in place until 1814 when the order was fully restored.

Today, there are about 19,000 Jesuits in the world.[35]

Nuns and Convents

So far most of our discussion has been focused on monks and monasteries. But just as important were the religious orders for women. The *nuns* in a *nunnery* or *convent* were presided over by an *abbess*. Since women were not allowed to be priests, a (male) priest would be assigned to serve priestly duties (communion, baptism, confession, etc.) in a nunnery or convent. A discussion of women that founded religious orders, monasteries or nunneries follows.

St. Paula (347-404)

St. Paula was a scholar and compatriot of St. Jerome, under whom she studied in both Rome and Jerusalem. (Jerome once said of her that she knew the Scriptures by memory). In Bethlehem, she financed construction of a monastery, a nunnery, and a hospice.

St. Olympias (c. 360/5–408)

Olympias of Constantinople was a wealthy disciple and patron of St. John of Chrysostom, Patriarch of Constantinople (398). She was ordained a deaconess by Bishop Nectarius of Constantinople, and later built a convent in Constantinople.

She remained a staunch supporter of St. John during his exile from Constantinople.

Melania the Younger (c. 383–439)

Melania the Younger was an acquaintance of both St. Augustine and St. Jerome. She built several monasteries and nunneries, in both Africa and in Jerusalem (one on the Mount of Olives). She served as the abbess of at least one of the nunneries that she built.

Her grandmother, Melania the Elder, was a patron of Rufinus, who translated Origen's writings into Latin. The Elder founded a monastery on Mt. of Olives.

St. Brigid of Ireland (c. 451/452–525)

St. Brigid founded the famous Convent of *Cill-Dara*, or Kildare, which grew into a cathedral city during her tenure as abbess. Some facts about St. Brigid include:

- Kildare was the first nunnery in Ireland.
- She may have held the power of a bishop during her tenure as abbess. Note in the following quote that she "appointed" a priest to her two religious houses. Typically, a local bishop would be in charge of appointing priests.
  - "She founded two monastic institutions, one for men, and the other for women, and appointed St. Conleth as spiritual pastor of them" (Catholic Encyclopedia[36])
- She was a compatriot of St. Patrick
- She is known as the "Patroness of Ireland"

Saint Scholastica (c. 480-547)

The (possibly twin) sister of St. Benedict, was the abbess of a convent at Plumbariola, located about 5 miles from Monte Cassino. In an incident recorded by St. Gregory the Great, her aging brother had come to visit her one day, and she wanted him to spend the night. He refused, saying that he couldn't spend the night outside his monastery. Scholastica prayed to God for a thunderstorm that would prevent her brother from leaving her, and the storm was delivered. Benedict was not able to leave his sister that night. Several days later, Scholastica died, and from his cell at Monte Cassino, Benedict saw her soul depart to heaven in the form of a dove.

As her brother founded the first Benedictine monastery, Scholastica founded the first Benedictine convent.

Hilda of Whitby (614-680)

As mentioned earlier, in 663, a great Synod was held at Whitby, under the patronage of Hilda of Whitby. The Synod of Whitby decided against Celtic calendar and tonsure, ensuring that Celtic monasticism in the future would have a more Roman flavor.

---

[36] http://www.newadvent.org/cathen/02784b.htm

After leading a "double monastery" (male and female) at Hartlepool, Hilda became abbess at Whitby Abbey, an abbey which would become famous under her leadership for learning and sanctity. Five future bishops trained in her double monastery community. Double monasteries were not uncommon in England during this period, and included Whitby, Ely, Much Wenlock, Bardney, Barking, Coldingham, Repton and Wimborne.

At her death, it is said that two miracles occurred. In Hackness, thirteen miles away, it was said that the monastery bells from Whitby could be heard. And a nun from Hackness claimed that she saw the soul of Hilda being taken to heaven.

Hilda of Whitby[37]

[37] Library of Congress LAMB, no. 473 (A size) [P&P];

St. Clare of Assisi (1194-1293)

St. Clare at Mission Santa Clara in California (Photo by Robert C. Jones)

St. Clare of Assisi, a disciple of St. Francis of Assisi, founded the *Order of Poor Ladies*, later known as the *Poor Clares*. She served as the abbess of the first community of the Poor Clares at San Damiano, in the Diocese of Assisi, for 40 years. Like her mentor St. Francis, she believed that those consecrated to Christ should live in complete poverty.

The Order spread quickly throughout Europe. In Spain, 47 convents were founded in the 13th century alone. The order still exists today:

> The Poor Clare Sisters number over 20,000 sisters throughout the world in 16 federations and in over 70 countries. Most monasteries have from four to thirteen members. Some have larger communities but the Poor Clare charisma [a power given by the Holy Spirit] is one of family and St. Clare guided us that small communites were much better to keep this family spirit than larger ones. So when a community gets to a certain number we

usually start new ones rather than just keep getting bigger. Just one of the differences you will see as you walk with us.[38]

St. Bridget of Sweden (c. 1303 – 1373)

Currier and Ives print of St. Bridget (between 1856 and 1907)[39]

St. Bridget of Sweden founded the *Established Order of the Most Holy Savior*, better known as the *Brigittines*. The order was made up of dual (male and female) monasteries, ruled by an abbess.

During her lifetime, Bridget was renowned for her visionary qualities, and writings about her revelations were revered during the Middle Ages. Like St. Catherine of Sienna, St. Bridget called for the Pope's return to Rome from Avignon, and worked tirelessly for church reforms. In a letter to Pope Gregory XI she said, "In thy curia arrogant pride rules, insatiable cupidity and execrable luxury."[40]

---

[38] http://poorclare.org/
[39] Library of Congress LC-USZC2-2981

The order dissipated during the 19th century, but was revived on a much smaller scale in 1976 (today they are renowned for their fudge).

> The Brigittine Order exists at present with thirteen monasteries of contemplative nuns and a congregation of contemplative-apostolic sisters whose mother-house is located in Rome, in the actual former dwelling of St. Birgitta.[41]

St. Teresa of Avila (1515-1582)

St. Teresa of Avila, a Carmelite nun, was a Christian mystic, a noted author, and the founder of a number of monasteries and convents. She is said to have experienced the transverberation, or spiritual piercing of her heart. About her book *Life written by herself* (1565), the Catholic Encyclopedia states that it "forms one of the most remarkable spiritual biographies with which only the *Confessions of St. Augustine* can bear comparison"[42].

Among the monasteries and convents founded by St. Teresa:

- The convent of Discalced[43] Carmelite Nuns of the Primitive Rule of St. Joseph at Avila (1562)
- Medina del Campo (1567)
- Malagon and Valladolid (1568)
- Toledo and Pastrana (1569)
- Salamanca (1570)
- Alba de Tormes (1571)
- Segovia (1574)
- Veas and Seville (1575)
- Caravaca (1576)
- Villanuava de la Jara and Palencia (1580)
- Soria (1581)
- Granada and Burgos (1582)[44]

---

[40] Reprinted in *Christian Women Writers of the Medieval World*, Katharina M. Wilson, Christian History, Issue 30, 1991

[41] http://www.brigittine.org/monks/ab0711.html

[42] http://www.newadvent.org/cathen/14515b.htm

[43] "Discalced" refers to the practice of going "unshod", or not wearing shoes, or only sandals

[44] List from *Catholic Encyclopedia* http://www.newadvent.org/cathen/14515b.htm

St. Teresa was canonized in 1622 by Gregory XV. She was also the first woman designated as a Doctor of the Church.

Spanish Missions in the New World

Date	Event
1521	Hernán Cortés conquers Mexico, and Franciscan priests begin baptizing Indian converts
1531	Appearance of Our Lady of Guadalupe in Mexico
1534	Father Vincente Valverde is nominated as the first bishop in Peru
1539	Fray Marcos de Niza, a Franciscan monk, crosses into what is now Arizona, from Mexico. He is known as the "first European West of the Rockies".
1540-1542	Coronado expedition to New Mexico
1565	First permanent parish established in America at St. Augustine, Florida
Late-16th century	Franciscan priests found a series of missions in Florida, and along the Gulf coast
1598-1680	A group of Franciscans establish the first Spanish mission in New Mexico at San Juan de los Caballeros (1598); 40 missions established in New Mexico by 1680
Early 18th century	Several missions established in Texas, including San Antonio de Valero (the Alamo)
1769	Junípero Serra founds Mission San Diego de Alcalá at San Diego. Eventually, a total of 21 missions would be established in California (the last in 1823).
1833-1834	Mexican government secularizes most missions in California (*An Act for the Secularization of the Missions of California*)

Monastic orders would have a large part in bringing the Christian religion to places in the New World such as Peru, Mexico, New Mexico, and California. Through the establishment of missions, patient monks preached to the Indians, provided food and shelter, and protected the Indians from secular forces that often wanted to exploit or enslave them. Most prominent among those orders creating the missions were the mendicant friars – Dominicans, and especially Franciscans.

In Mexico, Hernán Cortés had conquered Mexico (and the Aztec Empire) by 1521. Almost immediately, Franciscans began ministering to the indigenous Indians, starting first with the children, and later adults. The appearance of Our Lady of Guadalupe in 1531 was a powerful inducement for the Indians to convert. In 1537, via a papal Bull, indigenous Indians were given the same rights as white men.

In Peru, five Dominicans accompanied Pizarro in 1532 during the latter's conquest. In 1534, Father Vincente Valverde was nominated as the first Bishop in Peru (of Cuzco). In time, other monastic orders, including the Franciscans, the Augustinians, and the Jesuits would make their mark in Peru, building churches, monasteries, nunneries and schools. As in other areas of the New World, it was often the priests that stood as the only bulwark against the Spanish military seizing the indigenous Indians (Inca) for use as slaves.

The Inquisition was instituted in Peru (Lima) in 1570, and was not totally abolished until 1820. It should be noted that, in general, the Inquisition in Peru and Mexico were targeted towards Spanish "heretics" in the New World, and not towards the Indians.

San Francisco Cathedral in Cuernavaca, Mexico. This Franciscan monastery was founded by Cortez in 1529 (Photo by Robert C. Jones)

From their base in Mexico, missionaries starting moving northward into what would one day become the southwestern part of the United States, into Texas, New Mexico, Arizona, and, most prominently, California. In Lochiel, Arizona, a town on the border with Mexico, is a small isloated monument to Fray Marcos de Niza, a Franciscan monk, and the "first European West of the Rockies" (1539). He is probably the first white man to enter what is now Arizona/New Mexico.

Monument to Fray Marcos, located near Lochiel, Arizona. The marker reads, "By this valley of San Rafael, Fray Marcos de Niza, vice-commissary of the Franciscan order, and delegate of the viceroy in Mexico entered Arizona. The first European west of the Rockies. April 12, 1539". (Photo by Robert C. Jones)

Shortly thereafter, Coronado (1540-1542) journeyed into the same area, with Father Marcos as a guide. After Coronado went back to Mexico, three Franciscans remained behind to minister to the Indians. Juan de Padilla, Juan de la Cruz and Luis de Escalona became the first martyrs in what is now the United States, after being murdered by the Indians in New Mexico. A Franciscan expedition in 1581-82 met a similar fate.

Finally, in 1598, a group of Franciscans made the first Spanish mission in New Mexico at San Juan de los Caballeros. According to the Catholic Encyclopedia, by 1608 "8000 Indians had been converted. By

1617 the Franciscans had built eleven churches and converted 14,000 Indians."[45]

In 1680, an Indian revolt broke out (probably targeted toward the Spanish political rulers, rather than the friars), and all 33 missions extant at the time were destroyed. New Mexico was retaken by the Spanish in 1691-1695, and the Franciscan missions again flourished.

By the end of the 18th century, the missions in New Mexico were in decline. By the time of the expansion of the United States into New Mexico in 1848, the mission system was pretty much gone.

The interior of the *Church of the Immaculate Conception*, built starting in 1628, in Quarai, New Mexico. The church and mission were administered by three priests. Although there were 658 people living at Quarai in 1641, by 1678, the site was deserted, as drought, famine, and Apache attacks took their toll. (Photo by Robert C. Jones)

---

[45] http://www.newadvent.org/cathen/11001a.htm

The pueblo/mission complex known as Abo is located about 30 miles SE of Albuquerque, New Mexico. The site was inhabited by Pueblo (*Tompiro*) Indians for about 500 years before Spanish Franciscans began converting the Indians in 1622. The sandstone *San Gregorio de Abo* church was completed in the late 1620s, with later enlargements completed in 1651. The 132-foot church was built with buttresses, similar to Medieval Gothic cathedrals. (Photo by Robert C. Jones)

Statue of Father Junípero Serra, Mission Carmel, California (Photo by Robert C. Jones)

Perhaps the most famous monk in the New World was Father Junípero Serra (1713 - 1784), who helped found the system of 21 missions in California in the 18th century. Father Serra joined the Franciscan order in 1530, and eventually earned a doctorate in theology. Although stricken with a serious leg injury, in 1769 he accompanied Gaspar de Portolá on an expedition to California. On July 16, 1769, he founded the first of twenty-one California missions, Mission San Diego de Alcalá. He would go on to establish missions at San Carlos (1770), San Antonio (1771), San Gabriel (1771), and San Luis Obispo (1772).

As mentioned, eventually there were 21 missions, stretching from San Diego to Sonoma (north of San Francisco).

- Mission San Diego de Alcala (1769)
- Mission San Carlos Borroméo de Carmelo (1770)
- Mission San Antonio de Padua (1771)
- Mission San Gabriel Arcángel (1771)
- Mission San Luis Obispo (1772)
- Mission San Francisco de Asís (1776)
- Mission San Juan Capistrano (1776)
- Mission Santa Clara de Asís (1777)
- Mission San Buenaventura (1782)
- Mission Santa Barbara (1786)
- Mission La Purisíma Concepción (1787)
- Mission Santa Cruz (1791)
- Mission Nuestra Señora de la Soledad (1791)
- Mission San José (1797)
- Mission San Juan Bautista (1797)
- Mission San Miguel de Arcángel (1797)
- Mission San Fernando Rey de España (1797)
- Mission San Luis Rey de Francia (1798)
- Mission Santa Inés (1804)
- Mission San Rafael Arcángel (1817)
- Mission San Francisco de Solano (1823)

Mission Carmel, California was founded by Father Junípero Serra in 1770. Mission Carmel reached its population peak in 1794, when it had an Indian population of 927. By 1823, the population had dwindled to 381, and in 1834, the mission was secularized. (Photo by Robert C. Jones)

Photo of the church at Mission Santa Clara. Founded in 1777 by Fr. Tomas de la Pena, this Franciscan mission baptized over 8500 Indians, the most of any Spanish mission. Santa Clara College was founded here in 1851 by Jesuit Priest John Nobili, the first college in the State of California. (Photo by Robert C. Jones)

Cloister walk at Mission Carmel, California (Photo by Robert C. Jones)

Mission San Jose is located in the southeastern portion of Fremont, California. Founded on June 11, 1797 by Padre Fermin Francisco de LaSuen, Mission San Jose was the 14th of 21 Spanish missions to be built in California. At its peak, Mission San Jose had 150 buildings, controlled huge tracts of land in what is now East Bay, and had large amounts of livestock. (In 1832, 12,000 cattle, 13,000 horses, and 12,000 sheep were on the books). The Mission Church, first constructed as a permanent structure in 1809, was destroyed by the great earthquake of 1868, after having had its buttresses removed for aesthetic purposes the year before. The church was reconstructed between 1982-1985. The bells in the church tower are original, as is the adobe structure next to the church. (Photo by Robert C. Jones)

The Medieval Monastery

The monastic day was divided into seven "hours" by the Rule of Benedict (*opus dei*, or the "time of God"). While the names assigned to these hours, and the times they were practiced differed slightly from order to order, from country to country, and from season to season, a generic list of the daily rule follows:

- Vigils – early morning (typically 2:00)
- Lauds ("praises") – first light
- Prime – sunrise
- Terce – around 9:00 a.m.
- Sext/nones – noon
- Vespers – 4:30
- Compline – dusk (to "complete" the hours); afterwards, the monks retired to bed

Processional doorway from the cloister into the nave, at Lilleshall Abbey, England (Augustinian Canons). The double recess to the right was probably used to store books. (Photo by Robert C. Jones)

The hours were typically celebrated in the monastic church (see next section), in the monk's *choir*, a set of facing chairs at the top of the cross in a typical abbey church. Prayers, and recitation of the Psalms (often sung in Plain Chant) were the order of the day. Mass typically occurred only on Sundays, often being proceeded by a grand procession of the monks into the abbey church.

Depending on the order, the waking moments not spent following the seven "hours" might be spent in study, or manual work (most orders except the Carthusians and Cluniacs). Also, monks typically met together every day for a meeting known as the Chapter. At Chapter, the abbot presided over the Order, discussing news of the day, dealing with disciplinary problems, etc.

Monks typically slept in a common dormitory called a *dorter*, and had meals in common in the *refectory*. Silence was typically observed during meals, with a single reader intoning from the Lives of the Saints, the Church Fathers (especially Augustine, Jerome, Ambrose and Gregory) and the Bible.

Monastic Buildings

Ruins of Cistercian monastery Rievaulx Abbey (1132), North Yorkshire, England
(Photo by Robert C. Jones)

Monasteries were typically self-contained miniature cities, providing everything the community needed for day to day activities. The heart of the monastery was the abbey church, which was typically laid out on an east-west axis (long part of the cross), with the transepts (short part of the cross) going north-south at the east end. The high altar was usually in the chancel, east of the transepts (top of the cross) This was the area used by the monks for reciting the daily hours (the *monk's choir*). In England, the nave (western end of long arm) was used by townspeople (Benedictine monasteries). In Cistercian abbey churches, the nave was used by lay-brothers.

Below are descriptions of common buildings and architectural features in a monastery.

Cellarium – storehouse of monastery, often located under the dorter

Cellarium at Fountains Abbey, a former Cistercian monastery in North Yorkshire
(Photo by Robert C. Jones)

Chancel – east part of church (top of cross). Location of high altar and the monk's choir.

Chancel at Canterbury Cathedral Priory, a former Benedictine house, in England (Photo by Robert C. Jones)

Chapter House – building for general meetings of the monks with their abbot; it sometimes also contained the graves of abbots.

Ruins of the ornate Chapter House at Haughmond Abbey, England (Augustinian Canons) (Photo by Robert C. Jones)

Cloister – most monastic buildings surrounded a square in the center of the Abbey called the *cloister* (Latin *claustrum* – closed in). The open middle part of the cloister was known as the *garth*. It was often used to grow vegetables. The outside perimeter of the cloister often contained a vaulted walkway. In many monasteries, this walkway was closed in, and was used for used for reading, studying, and, most importantly, the copying of manuscripts.

Exterior view of the Cloister walk at Canterbury Cathedral (Photo by Robert C. Jones)

The south cloister walk of Mulchelney Abbey (Benedictine) in England. Cloister walks often contained individual carrels for monks to copy and illustrate manuscripts. Note the excellent light source. (Photo by Robert C. Jones)

Crypt – typically located under the monastic church; often the burial place of saints.

Crypt at Canterbury Cathedral (Photo by Robert C. Jones)

Dorter – sleeping quarters for monks (lay brothers had separate quarters). In England, in the 12th century, dorters were often laid out in barracks style. By the 14th century, many monasteries had erected partitions for privacy.

In some orders, especially those in which silence was enforced almost all of the time, communal sleeping arrangements were not allowed. Monks were assigned individual *cells* to live in. The Carthusians were an example of such an order.

Magnificent *dorter* at Cleeve Abbey, an English Cistercian house founded in 1198 (Photo by Robert C. Jones)

Mount Grace Priory, in North Yorkshire, was a Carthusian monastery, founded in 1398. Shown is an individual cell for a monk. Note the food hatch through which the monks received their food. This was to discourage talking during the delivery of the meal. (Photo by Robert C. Jones)

Flying buttress – an external stone arch used to help support the weight of the walls and roof of an abbey church

The flying buttress made the great medieval churches possible. This one is at Winchester Cathedral (1076), a former Benedictine Monastery. (Photo by Robert C. Jones)

Frater – (a.k.a. refectory) – the common dining hall, which often had a pulpit for readings during meals. Fraters were typically located close to the kitchen, where food was prepared.

Refectory ceiling at Cleeve Abbey (Photo by Robert C. Jones)

Rare photo of the Abbot's Kitchen, at Glastonbury Abbey, Somerset, England, in the snow (Photo by Robert C. Jones)

Galilee – westward extension of the nave

Ruins of the galilee at Glastonbury Abbey, Somerset, England (Photo by Robert C. Jones)

Gatehouse – where the porter could great visitors to the abbey

Gatehouse at the Cistercian Cleeve Abbey, Somerset, England. Cleeve was completed in 1198, and dissolved in 1537. (Photo by Robert C. Jones)

Rere-dorter – lavatories; also known as garderobe, *domus neccaria*

Rere-dorter at Cluniac monastery Castle Acre Priory (Norfolk, England) (Photo by Robert C. Jones)

Rood screen – stone partition with altars in front of it dividing the nave from the monk's choir

Transepts – North and South part of the church (short part of the cross). Often contained one or more chapels.

Overhead view of the transepts of Rievaulx Abbey, North Yorkshire, England (Photo by Robert C. Jones)

Warming house – building where a fire was kept burning all winter (often under the dorter)

The Decline of Monasticism

The reasons for the decline of monasticism as a major force in Western Christendom are many and varied. This section will examine some of them in roughly chronological order.

The Black Death

The Black Death, the Medieval name for either bubonic or pneumonic plague, raged through Europe from 1347 to 1351. Various estimates of the death toll range from one quarter to one third of the population of Europe. The monasteries were not immune from this pandemic. St. Albans in Britain, for example, lost 47 monks and an abbot in a short time. Many monasteries never fully recovered from the devastation of the Plague. This was especially true because by the time the Black Death hit, the period of the greatest fervor for the ideal of monasticism in Europe was already past.

Laxness in the Monastery

As previously mentioned, the story of Western monasticism in the Middle Ages was one of a cycle of laxness/reform. By the 13th and 14th centuries, the reform spirit had pretty much been overrun by the extreme wealth of various abbeys (and whole orders). Monasteries were often viewed as being oppressive rulers and landlords by the local populaces (during the Peasants Revolt of 1381 in England, there were peasant attacks on Bury St. Edmunds and St. Albans.) Local bishops and clerics were often jealous of their monastic neighbors, many of whom answered only to the pope. The mendicant movement of the early 13th century, so promising in its early manifestations, eventually became lax and was characterized by idleness. By the time of Chaucer's *Canterbury Tales* in 1380, monks and friars had often become objects of ridicule, as these portraits from the Prologue of Chaucer's famous work show:

THE MONK
Where this brave monk was of the cell.
The rule of Maurus or Saint Benedict,
By reason it was old and somewhat strict,
This said monk let such old things slowly pace
And followed new-world manners in their place...

What? Should he study as a madman would
Upon a book in cloister cell? Or yet
labour with his hands and swink and sweat,
As Austin bids? How shall the world be served?...

Now certainly he was a fine prelate:
He was not pale as some poor wasted ghost.
A fat swan loved he best of any roast.
His palfrey was as brown as is a berry....

THE FRIAR
A friar there was, a wanton and a merry,
A limiter, a very festive man...

Gently absolved too, leaving naught of dread.
He was an easy man to give penance
When knowing he should gain a good pittance;
For to a begging friar, money given
Is sign that any man has been well shriven...

In towns he knew the taverns, every one,
And every good host and each barmaid too-
Better than begging lepers, these he knew...

He was the finest beggar of his house;
A certain district being farmed to him,
None of his brethren dared approach its rim...[46]

The Reformation

Perhaps the greatest contributor to the downfall of monasticism in the Middle Ages was the Protestant Reformation. Martin Luther, a former monk himself, wrote heatedly against his former profession. And Henry VIII of England, in a short 4-year period, wiped out 800 monasteries.

The Philosophical Issue

As earlier noted, a nagging question had dogged monasticism from its very beginning in the deserts of Egypt – if being a monk brought one closer to God (and closer to salvation), did that mean that monks

---

[46] Canterbury Tales Prologue, Geoffrey Chaucer, Reprinted by World Library, 1996

were "better" than normal Christians? Were there two classes of Christians – one purer than the other?

Martin Luther strongly rejected the notion that monks were "holier" than normal Christians. And he added another reason for rejecting monasticism – he felt that it smacked of salvation by works.

> As monastic vows directly conflict with the first chief article, they must be absolutely abolished. For it is of them that Christ says, Matthew 24:5, 23 ff.: I am Christ, etc. For he who makes a vow to live as a monk believes that he will enter upon a mode of life holier than ordinary Christians lead, and wishes to earn heaven by his own works not only for himself, but also for others; this is to deny Christ. And they boast from their St. Thomas that a monastic vow is equal to Baptism. This is blasphemy (against God). (*The Smalcald Articles,* Martin Luther, 1537[47])

The Dissolution of the Monasteries

Byland Abbey was actually the fourth attempt by a group of Cistercian monks to found a monastery in a 43 year period, starting in 1134. The remains of the last (successful) attempt, Byland Abbey, are located in the extreme southwest corner of the North Yorkshire Moors. At the time of the dissolution in 1538, the number of monks was 25. The photos shows modern Anglican priests beginning their procession into the church ruins for a Sunday afternoon service. (Photo by Robert C. Jones)

---

[47] Ages Software, 1998

Walsingham Priory was established in 1169 by an order of Augustinian Canons. It was dissolved in 1538 by Henry VIII. All that is left of the church is the towering east wall of the chancel. The undercroft of the dorter also survives, as well as part of the gatehouse. (Photo by Robert C. Jones)

In the period from 1527/29, King Henry VIII of England sought an annulment from the pope of his marriage to Catherine of Aragon. After repeated refusals, in 1534, Henry led the passage of the Acts of Supremacy, which established the Church of England with the King at its head. A by-product of this action was that monasticism was entirely wiped out from England within 6 years.

From 1536/40, Henry and his secretary Thomas Cromwell dissolved 800 monasteries, and confiscated 200,000 pounds for the crown. In 1500, England had 10,000 monks and 2,000 nuns. By the end of 1540, they were all gone – most of them petitioned off by the crown. A few, such as Abbot Richard Whiting, the last abbot (1525 – 1539) of the great Benedictine monastery at Glastonbury, were executed.

Protestant Monks?

While in general, Protestants disapproved of the monastic ideal, there were a few curious exceptions. One was a group called the Seventh Day German Baptists, who built a medieval-style monastery in Pennsylvania's Lancaster County in 1732. Founded by a German mystic named Conrad Beissel, the faith incorporated such diverse elements of theology as Anabaptist, Dunkard, Rosicrucian, Catholic, Mystic, and Jewish.

The community was divided into three main groups. The married householders, who lived in single housing units near the Cloister, and the celibate Brothers and Sisters, who lived in the Cloister buildings themselves. *Ephrata Cloister* was basically self-sufficient, and like its medieval European counterparts, was the educational, industrial, spiritual and charitable center of the area in which it was located. At its peak, the order had over 300 members. While the last of the celibates died in 1814, the order itself survived until 1934.

The *Sister's House* at Ephrata Cloister, sleeping quarters for the celibate sisters

Would-be monk in the Ephrata Cloister *Solitary House*, which was used to house brothers who did not wish to live in the main dorter (Photo by Robert C. Jones)

The French Revolution

While monasticism was essentially wiped out in England in the 16th century by Henry VIII, it took until the late 18th century for a similar event to happen in France – this time, the catalyst was the French Revolution. The French government during the Revolution confiscated most church property, and priests and bishops were required to swear an oath to the new order or face dismissal (Civil Constitution of 1790). In 1790, the Cistercian and Cluniac orders were suppressed.

Political cartoon showing "a group of ecclesiastical figures departing a church with what remains of their belongings (following the November 1789 decree by the National Assembly regarding church property)"[48]

[48] Library of Congress LC-USZC2-3593

Western Monasticism Today

There are various estimates of the number of Western monastics in the world today. Mayeul de Dreuille in his book *From East to West: A History of Monasticism* estimates that there are 17,525 monks in the Roman Catholic Church today, and 25,820 nuns/sisters.[49] Interestingly enough, the United States has been an especially fertile ground for modern day monastics – the Benedictines, for example, have 30 monasteries in the United States. So the monastic ideal has hardly disappeared. However, unlike in the Middle Ages when monasticism had a terrific impact on the legal, governmental, educational, and spiritual lives of the people in the areas in which monasteries were located (and on Europe itself), today monasteries and their inhabitants tend to be rather low key. Modern monasteries are often connected to schools or hospitals, and are often focused on charity as their main *raison d'être*.

Trappist Monastery of the Holy Spirit in Conyers, Georgia (Photo by Robert C. Jones)

---

[49] *From East to West: A History of Monasticism*, Mayeul de Dreuille OSB, Crossroad Publishing, 1999

Conclusion

In the 2,000-year-old history of the Christian Church, monasticism had a long reign as a key (perhaps *the* key) form of expressing Christianity in the West. From the 6th century, when the Rule of Benedict was written, until the 16th and 18th centuries, when the monasteries were suppressed in England and France (respectively), monasticism was considered to be the "highest" form of Christianity. While we as Protestants today may disagree with the idea of two kinds of Christians (and the idea of salvation by works), we cannot help but admire the ideals of monasticism when it was at its best – as practiced by such great leaders as Saints Augustine, Benedict, Bernard, and Dunstan.

Appendix A – Characteristics of the Essenes

When I have taught this material as a class, one of the most popular sections is the one that discusses the Essenes, and possible similarities between the Essenes and later Christian monastics. In this appendix, we examine more about the "monastic" practices of the Essenes, examining First Century secular historians as well as the Dead Sea Scrolls (which may have been written by the Essenes). Were the Essenes the first monks in Judeo-Christian tradition?

First Century Secular Historians

Philo of Alexandria (15/10 B.C. – 45/50 A.D.)

> "...and yet no one, not even of those immoderately cruel tyrants, nor of the more treacherous and hypocritical oppressors was ever able to bring any real accusation against the multitude of those called Essenes or Holy. But everyone being subdued by the virtue of these men, looked up to them as free by nature, and not subject to the frown of any human being, and have celebrated their manner of messing together, and their fellowship with one another beyond all description in respect of its mutual good faith, which is an ample proof of a perfect and very happy life."
> (*Every Good Man is Free*, Philo of Alexandria, C.D. Yonge translation, 1854[50])

Philo of Alexandria was a noted Jewish philosopher in the first half of 1st Century A.D. He was noted for his Greek (Hellenized) religious philosophy, sometimes referred to as *neoplatonism*.

Philo comes into our story here because he wrote several pages about the Essenes in his work *Every Good Man Is Free*. Other than (possibly) the Dead Sea Scrolls, it is the oldest significant extant description of the Essenes, pre-dating Josephus by several decades.

Key aspects of Philo's description of the Essenes follow.

---

[50] *Every Good Man is Free*, Philo of Alexandria, C.D. Yonge translation, 1854

- **There were about 4,000 Essenes** - "...in number something more than four thousand in my opinion."[51]
- **They didn't sacrifice animals** - "...not sacrificing living animals..."[52]
- **Study was an important part of their daily routine** – "...but studying rather to preserve their own minds in a state of holiness and purity..."[53]
- **They lived in remote or rural areas** - "These men, in the first place, live in villages, avoiding all cities on account of the habitual lawlessness of those who inhabit them..."[54]
- **Their goal was not to accumulate wealth** - "Of these men, some cultivating the earth, and others devoting themselves to those arts which are the result of peace, benefit both themselves and all those who come in contact with them, not storing up treasures of silver and of gold, nor acquiring vast sections of the earth out of a desire for ample revenues, but providing all things which are requisite for the natural purposes of life". [55]
- **They were pacifists** - "Among those men you will find no makers of arrows, or javelins, or swords, or helmets, or breastplates, or shields; no makers of arms or of military engines; no one, in short, attending to any employment whatever connected with war, or even to any of those occupations even in peace which are easily perverted to wicked purposes..."[56]
- **They didn't engage in commerce** – "...for they are utterly ignorant...of all commercial dealings..."[57]
- **They didn't believe in slavery** - "...and there is not a single slave among them, but they are all free..."[58]
- **The Sabbath was holy; there was a hierarchy based on age** - "Now these laws they are taught at other times, indeed, but most especially on the seventh day, for the seventh day is accounted sacred, on which they abstain from all other employments, and

---

[51] *Ibid*
[52] *Ibid*
[53] *Ibid*
[54] *Ibid*
[55] *Ibid*
[56] *Ibid*
[57] *Ibid*
[58] *Ibid*

frequent the sacred places which are called synagogues, and there they sit according to their age in classes, the younger sitting under the elder, and listening with eager attention in becoming order."[59]

- **They were especially pious** - "They also furnish us with many proofs of a love of virtue, such as abstinence from all covetousness of money, from ambition, from indulgence in pleasures, temperance, endurance, and also moderation, simplicity, good temper, the absence of pride, obedience to the laws, steadiness, and everything of that kind; and, lastly, they bring forward as proofs of the love of mankind, goodwill, equality beyond all power of description, and fellowship, about which it is not unreasonable to say a few words."[60]

- **They lived communally** - "...they all dwell together in companies, the house is open to all those of the same notions, who come to them from other quarters..."[61]

- **They had no personal possessions** - "...their expenses are all in common; their garments belong to them all in common; their food is common, since they all eat in messes...For whatever they, after having been working during the day, receive for their wages, that they do not retain as their own, but bring it into the common stock, and give any advantage that is to be derived from it to all who desire to avail themselves of it".[62]

- **They took care of their sick and aged** - "...and those who are sick are not neglected because they are unable to contribute to the common stock..."[63]

Flavius Josephus (37 A.D. (?) - 100 A.D.)

> "For there are three philosophical sects among the Jews. The followers of the first of whom are the Pharisees; of the second the Sadducces; and the third sect, who pretends to a severer discipline, and called Essenes. These last are Jews by birth, and seem to have a greater affection for

---

[59] *Ibid*
[60] *Ibid*
[61] *Ibid*
[62] *Ibid*
[63] *Ibid*

one another than the other sects have." (*Jewish Wars*, Flavius Josephus, Book 2 Chapter 8, Translated by William Whiston[64])

Flavius Josephus was a Jewish aristocrat that led rebel troops against the Romans in Galilee during the First Jewish Revolt (66-73 A.D.) He later betrayed the Jews, and served the Romans. In his retirement as a Roman gentleman farmer, he wrote two massive historical works - *The Jewish War* and *Jewish Antiquities*. He discusses the Essenes in both works, and, curiously enough, in far more detail than he discusses the Pharisees or Sadducees, both of which are much better known religious sects to modern day Christians.

A summary of the writings of Josephus about the Essenes follows.

- **They believed in predestination**- "But the sect of the Essenes affirm, that fate governs all things, and that nothing befalls men but what is according to its determination." (*Jewish Antiquities*, Book 13, Chapter 5[65])
- **They believed in life after death** – "The doctrine of the Essenes is this: That all things are best ascribed to God. They teach the immortality of souls, and esteem that the rewards of righteousness are to be earnestly striven for..." (*Jewish Antiquities*, Book 18 Chapter 1[66])
- **At some point, they had been cast out of temple worship** – "... and when they send what they have dedicated to God into the temple, they do not offer sacrifices, because they have more pure lustrations of their own; on which account they are excluded from the common court of the temple, but offer their sacrifices themselves..." (*Jewish Antiquities*, Book 18 Chapter 1[67])
- **All possessions were held in common** – "...that institution of theirs which will not suffer anything to hinder them from having all things in common; so that a rich man enjoys no more of his own wealth than he who hath nothing at all..."[68]

---

[64] *The Works of Josephus*, Translated by William Whiston, 1736
[65] *Ibid*
[66] *Ibid*
[67] *Ibid*
[68] *Ibid*

- **The Essenes were 4,000 in number** - "There are about four thousand men that live in this way..." (*Jewish Antiquities*, Book 18 Chapter 1[69])
- **They didn't marry** – "They neglect wedlock, but choose out other persons' children, while the are pliable, and fit for learning; and esteem them to be of their kindred, and form them according to their own manners." (*Jewish Wars*, Book 2 Chapter 8[70])
- **They dwell in multiple cities** – "They have no certain city but many of them dwell in every city; and if any of their sect come from other places, what they have lies open for them, just as if it were their own; and they go into such as they never knew before, as if they had been ever so long acquainted with them." (*Jewish Wars*, Book 2 Chapter 8[71])
- **They did occasionally arm themselves** – "For which reason they carry nothing with them when they travel into remote parts, though still they take their weapons with them, for fear of thieves." (*Jewish Wars*, Book 2 Chapter 8[72])
- **Like Medieval monks, their day seems to have been divided into "hours"** – "After this [sunrise] every one of them are sent away by their curators, to exercise some of those arts wherein they are skilled, in which they labor with great diligence till the fifth hour." (*Jewish Wars*, Book 2 Chapter 8[73])
- **They practiced water purification** – "...and when they have clothed themselves in white veils, they then bathe their bodies in cold water. And after this purification is over..." (*Jewish Wars*, Book 2 Chapter 8[74])
- **They eat communally** – "...they go, after a pure manner, into the dining room; as into a certain holy temple, and quietly set themselves down; upon which the baker lays them loaves in order; the cook also brings a single place of one sort of food, and sets it before every one of them..." (*Jewish Wars*, Book 2 Chapter 8[75])

---

[69] *Ibid*
[70] *Ibid*
[71] *Ibid*
[72] *Ibid*
[73] *Ibid*
[74] *Ibid*
[75] *Ibid*

- **They don't swear oaths...** - "...whatsoever they say also is firmer than an oath; but swearing is avoided by them, and they esteem it worse than perjury; for they say, that he who cannot be believed without [swearing by] God, is already condemned." (*Jewish Wars*, Book 2 Chapter 8[76])
- **Except when they swear oaths** – "And before [a novitiate] is allowed to touch their common food, he is obliged to take tremendous oaths..." (*Jewish Wars*, Book 2 Chapter 8[77])
- **They were scholars** – "They also take great pains in studying the writings of the ancients, and choose out of them what is most for the advantage of their soul and body". (*Jewish Wars*, Book 2 Chapter 8[78])
- **There was a three year probationary period for admittance into the sect** – "But now, if any one hath a mind to come over to their sect, he is not immediately admitted, but he is prescribed the same method of living which they use, for a year...after this demonstration of his fortitude, his temper is tried two more years, and if he appear to be worthy, they then admit him into their society." (*Jewish Wars*, Book 2 Chapter 8[79])
- **They practiced excommunication** – "But for those that are caught in any heinous sins, they cast them out of their society; and he who is thus separated from them..." (*Jewish Wars*, Book 2 Chapter 8[80])
- **They had a judicial system** – "But in the judgments they exercise they are most accurate and just; nor do they pass sentence by the votes of a court that is fewer than a hundred. And as to what is once determined by that number, it is unalterable." (*Jewish Wars*, Book 2 Chapter 8[81])
- **They strictly observed the Sabbath** – "Moreover, they are stricter than any other of the Jews in resting from their labors on the seventh day; for they not only get their food ready the day before, that they may not be obliged to kindle a fire on that day, but they

---

[76] *Ibid*

[77] *Ibid*

[78] *Ibid*

[79] *Ibid*

[80] *Ibid*

[81] *Ibid*

will not remove any vessel out of its place, nor go to stool there-on." (*Jewish Wars*, Book 2 Chapter 8[82])

- **They had a hierarchical system** – "Now after the time of their preparatory trial is over, they are parted into four classes; and so far are the juniors inferior to the seniors, that if the seniors should be touched by the juniors, they must wash themselves, as if they had intermixed themselves with the company of a foreigner." (*Jewish Wars*, Book 2 Chapter 8[83])

- **They were brave in the face of adversity** – "...and indeed our war with the Romans gave abundant evidence what great souls they had in their trials, wherein, although they were tortured and dis-torted, burnt and torn to pieces, and went through all kinds of in-struments of torment, that they might be forced either to blas-pheme their legislator, or to eat what was forbidden them, yet could they not be made to do either of them, no, nor once to flat-ter their tormentors, or to shed a tear..." (*Jewish Wars*, Book 2 Chapter 8[84])

- **They were renowned for their prophetic abilities** – "There are also those among them who undertake to foretell things to come, by reading the holy books, and using several sorts of purifications, and being perpetually conversant in the discourses of the proph-ets; and it is but seldom that they miss in their predictions." (*Jew-ish Wars*, Book 2 Chapter 8[85]) [Note: Josephus mentions several Essenes with prophetic ability, including Judas, Manahem, and Si-mon]

- **There was more than one order of Essenes** – "Moreover, there is another order of Essenes, who agree with the rest as to their way of living, and customs, and laws, but differ from them in the point of marriage, as thinking that by not marrying they cut off the prin-cipal part of the human life, which is the prospect of succession; nay rather, that if all men should be of the same opinion, the whole race of mankind would fail."[86]

---

[82] *Ibid*
[83] *Ibid*
[84] *Ibid*
[85] *Ibid*
[86] *Ibid*

There is remarkable similarity between the descriptions of Philo and Josephus, even though they were written decades apart. There are a few discrepancies:

- Philo says they avoided cities; Josephus says they were "city dwellers"
- Philo says they were radical pacifists; Josephus says they carried weapons on trips to defend themselves

But all in all, remarkable agreement between the two historians, even down to the number of Essenes - 4,000.

Pliny the Elder (d. 79 A.D.)

Pliny the Elder led a varied life, serving as a cavalry commander in the Roman army, procurator of Spain, and commander of the fleet of the Bay of Naples. He was also a writer and scholar, and published his 39-book *Natural History* in 77 A.D. It is in this work that Pliny discusses the Essenes. Like Philo and Josephus, he discusses them with enthusiasm bordering on reverence.

> Lying on the west of the [Dead Sea], and sufficiently distant to escape its noxious exhalations, are the Esseni [Essenes], a people that live apart from the world, and marvelous beyond all others throughout the whole earth, for they have no women among them; to sexual desire they are strangers; money they have none; the palm-trees are their only companions. Day after day, however, their numbers are fully recruited by multitudes of strangers that resort to them, driven thither to adopt their usages by the tempests of fortune, and wearied with the miseries of life. Thus it is, that through thousands of ages, incredible to relate, this people eternally prolongs its existence, without a single birth taking place there; so fruitful a source of population to it is that weariness of life which is felt by others. Below this people was formerly the town of Engadda [Engedi], second only to Hierosolyma in the fertility of its soil and its groves of palm-trees; now, like it, it is another heap of ashes. Next to it we come to Masada, a fortress on a rock, not far from [the Dead Sea]. Thus much concerning Judea. (*The Natural History*, Pliny the Elder, Translated by John Bostock, M.D., F.R.S., H.T. Riley, Esq., B.A., Ed.[87])

---

[87] *The Natural History,* London. Taylor and Francis, Red Lion Court, Fleet Street. 1855

Here, finally, we hear a connection between the Essenes, the Judean desert, and the Dead Sea. Pliny also echoes Philo and Josephus in terms of identifying that the Essene "people" "have no women among them; to sexual desire they are strangers; money they have none..."

Pliny also underscores how a religious sect that doesn't believe in marriage propagates itself – "persons tired of life and driven thither by the waves of fortune to adopt their manner".

Note also the text "Below this people was formerly the town of Engadda [Engedi]". If one views that "below" means "south of", then it could be interpreted that this passage says "Engedi lies south of the Essenes [Qumran is north of Engedi]".

So, the Essenes sure sound like a bunch of monks, and some of them even live in the desert, which brings us to 1947-48, and the discovery of the Dead Sea Scrolls...

The Dead Sea Scrolls

The Dead Sea Scrolls caves, near Qumran[88]

---

[88] Library of Congress LC-DIG-matpc-22896

Beginning in 1947-48, over 800 scrolls have been discovered in Judean desert caves, near the archaeological site of Qumran. Two hundred of the scrolls were ancient copies of Old Testament books (a 1,000 years older than the previously oldest extant copies of the Old Testament). What has been especially intriguing about the discovery was the content of the other 600 scrolls – previously unknown Psalms, Old Testament commentaries (Isaiah, Hosea, Nahum, Habakkuk), apocalyptic writings, and a set of scrolls that seemed to define the laws of an unknown Jewish sect.

Father Roland de Vaux, who excavated the Qumran site in 1951-56, first promulgated the view of the site as an Essene monastery, and that the scrolls were the library of the Essenes. This view has since been challenged by others that 1) say that there is no evidence of any connection between Qumran and the scrolls themselves and 2) the wide diversity of viewpoints contained within the scrolls make it more likely that the scrolls are the library of the Temple of Jerusalem, brought to the Judean desert for safe-keeping during the Roman siege in 68/70 A.D., and then forgotten.

I don't necessarily view these two viewpoints as mutually exclusive. If our goal is to better understand the Essenes, the question is, "Are there any Essene documents among the Qumran Scrolls?", as opposed to "Is this an Essene Library or a Temple Library?" (Assumedly, both libraries would contain documents from diverse sects and philosophies).

In answer to the question posed above - "Are there any Essene documents among the Qumran Scrolls?" – the answer is probably yes. The two most important to adding to our understanding of the Essenes are *The Manual of Discipline* (a.k.a. the *Community Rule*) and the *Damascus Document*. Both appear to be the constitution of an unnamed Jewish sect – dare we even say, an unknown Jewish *monastic* sect. There is enough commonality between the two documents to assume they are from the same group – although they may represent slightly different points on the timeline regarding the development of the sect. (Note: Some people have postulated that the *Manual of Discipline* contains the rules for the celibate monastic branch of the sect, and the *Damascus Document* contains the rules for the lay members of the sect. Josephus in *Jewish Wars* mentioned two such branches.)

Manual of Discipline

> "And this is the order for the men of the community who have offered themselves to turn from all evil and to lay hold of all that he commanded according to his will, to be separated from the congregation of the men of error, to become a community in law and in wealth, answering when asked by the sons of Zadok, the priests who keep the covenant..." (*Manual of Discipline*, Translated by Millar Burrows[89])

The *Manual of Discipline* (also known as the *Community Rule*) was originally found in two pieces in Cave 1. When combined, it appears to be an almost complete document. It measures about 9.5" x 6'. Underscoring the potential significance of the document is the fact that ten additional (fragmentary) copies were found in Cave 4.

The curious title was given to the book by Millar Burrows, who, as director of the American School of Oriental Research in 1947, was one of the first to examine the scroll. Burrows thought that its "combination of liturgical directions with rules concerning procedure in the meetings of the group and the personal conduct of the members" reminded him of a similar book used in the Methodist Church, called the Manual of Discipline.[90]

The document contains the rules, or the "constitution" of a mysterious religious order. It has been compared with the Christian *Didache* and *Apostolic Constitutions* of the 2nd-4th centuries.

The document appears to be in four parts, named by Burrows as "Entering the Convenant", "Two Spirits in Man", Rules of the Order", and "The Closing Psalm". From the first part:

> ...the order of the community; to seek God... to do what is good and upright before him as he commanded through Moses and through his ser-

---

[89] *The Dead Sea Scrolls*, Millar Burrows, The Viking Press, 1961
[90] *Ibid*

vants the prophets...to love all the sons of light, each according to his lot in the counsel of God, and to hate all the sons of darkness, each according to his guilt in vengeance of God. (*Manual Of Discipline*, Translated by Millar Burrows[91])

Damascus Document

The *Damascus Document*, so named because there are seven references to Damascus contained within, was first found in a Cairo *genizah* in 1897 by Solomon Schechter of Cambridge. Like the *Manual of Discipline*, multiple copies of the document were found among the Dead Sea Scrolls (at least ten). Also like the *Manual of Discipline*, the document describes a series of statutes regarding a mysterious religious order, which may have called itself the "sons of Zadok":

> The Sons of Zadok are the elect of Israel, those called by name, who will abide at the end of days. (*Manual of Discipline,* Translated by Millar Burrows[92])

The document is in two parts. Part One is a "History/Exhortation"; Part Two is the statutes or laws. Intriguingly, the Damascus Document refers to many of the same characters described in the Habakkuk and Psalms commentaries – The teacher of righteousness, the man of the lie, the preacher of the lie, etc. are all mentioned. Because of this similarity in characters, many people feel that the two must have been written by the same sect. The document also refers to "the decision of those who entered the new covenant in the land of Damascus", which could possibly refer to the foundation of the sect.

"The Sectarians"

None of the aforementioned documents that are seemingly Essene in origin identify the name of the group or sect that wrote them. The only seeming identification given in the texts is "the sons of light" or the "sons of Zadok" (possibly, the Chief Priest under Kings David and Solomon.)

As mentioned earlier, 1st century Jewish Historian Josephus tells us that there were three Jewish sects at the time of Jesus - was the

---

[91] *Ibid*
[92] *Ibid*

Qumran sect one of those three, or was it a group whose name is lost to history? What do the scrolls themselves tell us about the sect? Taking the *Damascus Document* and the *Manual of Discipline* together (and assuming that they are rules for the same sect), we might make some of the following statements about the sect:

- They were headed by a "superintendent" or "examiner", who seemed to be both teacher and Chief Financial Officer
- Judicial decisions were made by the assembled members of the group
- Apparently there was community ownership of property (However, the scrolls are a bit ambiguous on this point - the *Damascus Document* talks about 2 days wages from each person being given to the "poor and needy" each month. As mentioned previously, this could reflect that the *Damascus Document* is the set of rules for the Lay branch of the Essenes mentioned in Josephus).
- There appears to have been a required two-stage (one year each) probation period for entry into the sect
- They were very focused on ritual purity
- They believed that their purpose was to prepare the way of the Lord by the study of the Law

> When these things come to pass for the community in Israel, by these regulations they shall be separated from the midst of the session of the men of error to go to the wilderness to prepare there the way of the LORD...This is the study of the law, as he commanded through Moses... (*Manual of Discipline*, Translated by Millar Burrows[93])

- Prayer was an important element of their daily worship
- They were "a holy house for Israel, a foundation of the holy of holies for Aaron."
- Those that violated Mosaic law willfully were excommunicated
- They scrupulously obeyed the Sabbath
- There was some degree of hierarchy – "the lesser obeying the greater". "Priests and elders" were seated first in community meetings.

In terms of the theology of the sect:

---

[93] *Ibid*

- They believed in divine election (predestination)
- They appeared to have strong apocalyptic and eschatological views

> But God in the mysteries of his understanding and in his glorious wisdom has ordained a period for the ruin of error, and in the appointed time of punishment he will destroy it forever." (*Manual of Discipline*, Translated by Millar Burrows[94])

- They defined good and evil in terms of light and darkness
- Man is weak and utterly dependent on God
- Salvation appears to be through 1) the law 2) following the teacher of righteousness and 3) confessing before God "we have sinned"

> But all who hold fast to these ordinances, going out and coming in according to the law, and who listen to the voice of a teacher and confess before God, 'We have sinned...' who give ear to the voice of a teacher of righteousness...they shall prevail over all the sons of the world, and God will forgive them, and they shall see his salvation... (*Damascus Document*, Translated by Millar Burrows[95])

As one can tell from the list of attributes above, there are many similarities between the descriptions of the Essenes from Josephus/Philo, and the Dead Sea Scrolls "constitution" documents. There are enough similarities between Josephus/Philo and the scrolls to build a case for the Sectarians being Essenes, as demonstrated in following table.

Josephus/Philo	Dead Sea Scrolls
Abbreviations used: JA = *Jewish Antiquities*, JW = *Jewish Wars*, DD = *Damascus Document*, MOD = *Manual of Discipline*	
"Nor is there any one to be found among them who hath more than another; for it is a law among them, that those who come to them must let what they have be common to the whole order..." (JW, Book 2,	"If the lot determines that he is to be admitted to the community...his wealth and wages shall be put at the disposal of the man who has supervision over the wages of the masters." (MOD[98])

---

[94] *Ibid*

[95] *Ibid*

Josephus/Philo	Dead Sea Scrolls
Chapter 8[96]) "…their expenses are all in common; their garments belong to them all in common; their food is common…" (Philo of Alexandria[97])	
"They also have stewards appointed to take care of their common affairs, who every one of them have no separate business for any, but what is for the uses of them all…" (JW, Book 2, Chapter 8[99])	"And this is the order for the superintendent of the camp: He shall instruct the many in the works of God…and every one who is added to his congregation he shall examine him as to his works…and no man shall make an agreement for buying and selling unless he has told the superintendent who is in the camp…" (DD[100])
"But now if any one hath a mind to come over to their sect, he is not immediately admitted, but he is prescribed the same method of living which they use for a year… for after this demonstration of his fortitude, his temper is tried two more years; and if he appear to be worthy, they then admit him into their society…" (JW, Book 2, Chapter 8[101])	"When he has completed a year within the community, the masters shall be questioned about his affairs…the new member shall not touch the sacred drink of the masters until he has completed a second year among the community of men." (MOD[102])
"But for those that are caught in any heinous sins, they cast them out of their society." (JW, Book 2, Chapter 8[103])	"Any man of them who transgresses a word of the law of Moses overtly or with deceit shall be dismissed from the council of the community and shall not come back again." (MOD[104])
"…they pass sentence by the votes of a court that is fewer than a hun-	"And this is the order for the judges of the congregation: There shall be

[96] *The Works of Josephus*, Translated by William Whiston, 1736
[97] *Every Good Man is Free*, Philo of Alexandria, C.D. Yonge translation, 1854
[98] *The Dead Sea Scrolls*, Millar Burrows, The Viking Press, 1961
[99] *The Works of Josephus*, Translated by William Whiston, 1736
[100] *The Dead Sea Scrolls, Millar Burrows, The Viking Press, 1961*
[101] *The Works of Josephus*, Translated by William Whiston, 1736
[102] *The Dead Sea Scrolls*, Millar Burrows, The Viking Press, 1961
[103] *The Works of Josephus*, Translated by William Whiston, 1736
[104] *The Dead Sea Scrolls*, Millar Burrows, The Viking Press, 1961

Josephus/Philo	Dead Sea Scrolls
dred..." (JW, Book 2, Chapter 8[105])	as many as ten men chosen by the congregation according to the time." (DD[106]) "There shall be in the council of the community twelve men..." (MOD[107])
"Now after the time of their preparatory trial is over, they are parted into four classes; and so far are the juniors inferior to the seniors, that if the seniors should be touched by the juniors, they must wash themselves, as if they had intermixed themselves with the company of a foreigner." (JW, Book 2, Chapter 8[108]) "...they sit according to their age in classes, the younger sitting under the elder, and listening with eager attention in becoming order." (Philo[109])	"And this is the order of the session of all the camps: They shall be enrolled by their names; the priests first, the Levites second, the sons of Israel third, and the proselyte fourth." (DD[110])
"But the sect of the Essenes affirm, that fate governs all things..." (JA, Book 13, Chapter 5[111])	"To those whom God has chosen he has given them for an eternal possession..." (MOD[112])
"They also avoid spitting in the midst of them..." (JW, Book 2, Chapter 8[113])	"A man that spits into the midst of the session of masters shall be punished thirty days." (MOD[114])

[105] *The Works of Josephus,* Translated by William Whiston, 1736
[106] *The Dead Sea Scrolls*, Millar Burrows, The Viking Press, 1961
[107] *Ibid*
[108] *The Works of Josephus,* Translated by William Whiston, 1736
[109] *Every Good Man is Free*, Philo of Alexandria, C.D. Yonge translation, 1854
[110] *The Dead Sea Scrolls*, Millar Burrows, The Viking Press, 1961
[111] *The Works of Josephus,* Translated by William Whiston, 1736
[112] *The Dead Sea Scrolls*, Millar Burrows, The Viking Press, 1961
[113] *The Works of Josephus,* Translated by William Whiston, 1736
[114] *The Dead Sea Scrolls*, Millar Burrows, The Viking Press, 1961

Josephus/Philo	Dead Sea Scrolls
"A priest says grace before meat; and it is unlawful for any one to taste of the food before grace be said. The same priest, when he hath dined, says grace again after meat..." (JW, Book 2, Chapter 8[115])	"...the priest shall stretch out his hand first to pronounce a blessing with the first portion of the bread and the wine..." (MOD[116])
"Nor is there ever any clamor or disturbance to pollute their house, but they give every one leave to speak in their turn..." (JW, Book 2, Chapter 8[117])	"...so that each may render his opinion to the council of the community. A man shall not speak in the midst of his neighbor's words, before his brother finishes speaking" (MOD[118])

There are some differences between the Scroll writings, and those of Josephus and Philo. For example, Josephus tells us that the Essenes numbered about 4,000, and "they have no one certain city, but many of them dwell in every city" – certainly a different picture from this seemingly monastic desert sect. Also, the teacher of righteousness, who is so prominent in several of the scrolls, is not even hinted at in Josephus. Finally, there is no mention in Philo or Josephus (or Pliny) of the elaborate (364 day) calendar system used by the Scroll sectarians.

However, one must keep in mind that the *Manual of Discipline* and the *Damascus Document* date to 100-200 years earlier than the histories of Philo, Josephus, and Pliny the Elder. As in the United States today, there is less discussion of Founding Father George Washington than there was 100 years ago. It is quite possible that the Teacher of Righteousness was a hot topic in documents written within 20 years of the founding of the sect, but had faded in every day consciousness 150 years later. The same thing could be said about the calendar situation – hot topic in 100 B.C., but institutionalized, so not mentioned, in 60 A.D.

As far as the issue of "many of them dwell in every city", cited in Josephus, this is somewhat counterbalanced by Philo, who states

---

[115] *The Works of Josephus,* Translated by William Whiston, 1736
[116] *The Dead Sea Scrolls*, Millar Burrows, The Viking Press, 1961
[117] *The Works of Josephus,* Translated by William Whiston, 1736
[118] *The Dead Sea Scrolls*, Millar Burrows, The Viking Press, 1961

"these men, in the first place, live in villages, avoiding all cities on account of the habitual lawlessness of those who inhabit them", which would indicate that even in Philo's time, the Essenes inhabited more remote locations (some have suggested that Qumran was the center of Essenes, sort of like Citeaux would later be for the Christian Cistercians). And, of course, we have Pliny the Elder's comment that Essenes live "away from the western shore [of the Dead Sea], far enough to avoid harmful things, a people alone...companions of palm trees."

In summary, while not all of the 800 scrolls in the Dead Sea Scrolls are necessarily Essene in origin (for example, there are some scrolls that date back as early as 250 B.C.), the "sectarian" scrolls probably *are* Essene in origin.

Appendix B - Jewish Monks/Christian Monks

Assuming that the group we call the Essenes is the sect described in Philo, Josephus, Pliny, the *Damascus Document*, and the *Manual of Discipline*, we see remarkable similarities between this group, and later Christian monastics. In the table below we examine some of the rules and attributes of the Essenes that seem to closely parallel the later Christian monastic rules include:

Essenes	Christian monasticism
Abbreviations used: JA = *Jewish Antiquities*; JW = *Jewish Wars*; MOD = *Manual of Discipline*, Burrows translation	
They were headed by a "super-intendent" or "examiner", who seemed to be both teacher and Chief Financial Officer	Headed by an Abbot or prior, who had absolute authority - "He is believed to hold the place of Christ in the monastery, since he is addressed by a title of Christ." (*Rule of Benedict*, Chapter 2[119]) "Obey the prioress as a mother, giving her all due honor, that God may not be offended by your forgetting what you owe to her..." (*Letter 211*, A.D. 423, St. Augustine, Translated by the Rev. J. G. Cunningham, M.A.[120])
Judicial decisions were made by the assembled members of the group	Chapter house - "As often as anything important is to be done in the monastery, the abbot shall call the whole community together and himself explain what the business is; and after hearing the advice of the broth-ers, let him ponder it and follow what he judges the wiser course." (*Rule of Benedict*, Chapter 3[121])
"Nor is there any one to be found among them who hath	"Above all, this evil practice [private property] must be up-

[119] *The Order of St. Benedict*, The Liturgical Press, 1982
[120] *The Nicene and Post-Nicene Fathers First Series, Volume 1*, By Philip Schaff, editor
[121] *The Order of St. Benedict*, The Liturgical Press, 1982

Essenes	Christian monasticism
Abbreviations used: JA = *Jewish Antiquities*; JW = *Jewish Wars*; MOD = *Manual of Discipline*, Burrows translation	
more than another; for it is a law among them, that those who come to them must let what they have be common to the whole order..." (Josephus, JW, Book 2, Chapter 8[122]) "If the lot determines that he is to be admitted to the community...his wealth and wages shall be put at the disposal of the man who has supervision over the wages of the masters." (MOD[123])	rooted and removed from the monastery. We mean that without an order from the abbot, no one may presume to give, receive or retain anything as his own, nothing at all – not a book, writing tablets or stylus – in short, not a single item..." (*Rule of Benedict*, Chapter 33[124]) "Also call not anything the property of any one, but let all things be common property..." (*Letter 211*, A.D. 423, St. Augustine, Translated by the Rev. J. G. Cunningham, M.A.[125])
There appears to have been a required two-stage (one year each) probation period for entry into the sect "When he has completed a year within the community, the masters shall be questioned about his affairs...the new member shall not touch the sacred drink of the masters until he has completed a second year among the community of men." (MOD[126])	Novitiate periods of varying lengths were required – the Benedictines had a 12-month novitiate period "If after due reflection he promises to observe everything and to obey every command given him, let him be received into the community." (*Rule of Benedict*, Chapter 58[127])
Tended to live in remote areas or small villages	Tended to live in remote areas or small villages (especially Cistercians, Carthusians)
Prayer was an important element of their daily worship	Day divided into "hours" - Lauds, Prime, Terce, Sext, Nones, Vespers, Compline - in which prayer was an important element.

[122] *The Works of Josephus*, Translated by William Whiston, 1736
[123] *The Dead Sea Scrolls*, Millar Burrows, The Viking Press, 1961
[124] *The Order of St. Benedict*, The Liturgical Press, 1982
[125] *The Nicene and Post-Nicene Fathers First Series, Volume 1*, By Philip Schaff, editor
[126] *The Dead Sea Scrolls*, Millar Burrows, The Viking Press, 1961
[127] *The Order of St. Benedict*, The Liturgical Press, 1982

Essenes	Christian monasticism
Abbreviations used: JA = *Jewish Antiquities*; JW = *Jewish Wars*; MOD = *Manual of Discipline*, Burrows translation	
	"Seven times a day I praise you for your righteous laws." (Psalms 119:164, NIV)
Those that violated Mosaic law and the community rule willfully were excommunicated "Any man of them who transgresses a word of the law of Moses overtly or with deceit shall be dismissed from the council of the community and shall not come back again." (MOD[128])	Among the Benedictines, excommunication in degrees - Rebuking in front of the community, exclusion from table and oratory, shunning, "strokes of the rod", banishment from the community
"...they all dwell together in companies, the house is open to all those of the same notions, who come to them from other quarters..." (Philo[129])	"The monks are to sleep in separate beds...If possible, all are to sleep in one place...A lamp must be kept burning in the room until morning." (*Rule of Benedict*, Chapter 22[130])
"They neglect wedlock, but choose out other persons' children, while they are pliable, and fit for learning; and esteem them to be of their kindred, and form them according to their own manners." (Philo[131])	Monastic celibacy; children of nobleman (rarely the first born son) were often turned over to monasteries to be raised in the church
"...they shall eat in common and pray in common and deliberate in common..." (MOD[132])	Communal meals, communal observation of the "hours", Chapter house
"After this [sunrise] every one of them are sent away by their curators, to exercise some of those arts wherein they are skilled, in which they labor with great diligence till the fifth hour." (Josephus, JW, Book 2, Chapter	"Idleness is the enemy of the soul. Therefore, the brothers should have specified periods for manual labor as well as for prayerful reading." (*Rule of Benedict*, Chapter 48[134])

[128] *The Dead Sea Scrolls*, Millar Burrows, The Viking Press, 1961
[129] *Every Good Man is Free*, Philo of Alexandria, C.D. Yonge translation, 1854
[130] *The Order of St. Benedict*, The Liturgical Press, 1982
[131] *Every Good Man is Free*, Philo of Alexandria, C.D. Yonge translation, 1854
[132] *The Dead Sea Scrolls*, Millar Burrows, The Viking Press, 1961

Essenes	Christian monasticism
Abbreviations used: JA = *Jewish Antiquities*; JW = *Jewish Wars*; MOD = *Manual of Discipline*, Burrows translation	
8[133])	

Whether the rules of the Essenes were later emulated by St. Benedict or St. Augustine[135], or rather simply paralleled, we cannot say. But we can say that there were striking similarities between the "Jewish monks" of 2,000 years ago, and Medieval Christian monasticism.

---

[133] *The Works of Josephus,* Translated by William Whiston, 1736

[134] *Ibid*

[135] While the Dead Sea Scrolls wouldn't have been available to Benedict and Augustine, certainly the works of Josephus, Pliny the Elder, and Philo of Alexandria would have been available to both of them

Sources

Title	Author	Publisher	Date
Canterbury Tales Prologue	Geoffrey Chaucer	World Library	1996
Christian Women Writers of the Medieval World	Katharina M. Wilson	Christian History, Issue 30	1991
Dead Sea Scrolls, The	Millar Burrows	The Viking Press	1961
Early Church, The	Henry Chadwick	Dorset Press	1986
Every Good Man is Free	Philo of Alexandria, C.D. Yonge translation		1854
Flowering of the Middle Ages, The	Edited by Joan Evans	Bonanza Books	1985
From East to West: A History of Monasticism	Mayeul de Dreuille OSB	Crossroad Publishing	1999
Glastonbury Abbey: The Holy House at the Head of the Moors Adventurous	James P. Carley	The Boydell Press	1988
History of the Christian Church Vol. 5	Philip Schaff	Ages Software	1999
Holy Bible – New Revised Standard Version		Zondervan Publishing House	1989, 1993
Horizon Book of the Middle Ages, The	Norman Kotker; Morris Bishop	American Heritage/Bonanza Books	1984
Life in Medieval Times	Marjorie Rowling	Perigee Books	1968
Medieval and Renaissance World, The	General Editor: Esmond Wright	Hamlyn Publishing	1979
Medieval Monasteries of Great Britain	Lionel Butler & Chris Given-Wilson	Michael Joseph Limited	1979
Natural History, The	Pliny the Elder, Translated by John Bostock	Taylor and Francis	1855
Nicene and Post-Nicene Fathers First Series, Volume 1, The	Philip Schaff, editor	Ages Software	1999
Nicene And Post-	Philip Schaff, editor	Ages Soft-	1999

Title	Author	Publisher	Date
Nicene Fathers Second Series, Volumes 1&4, The		ware	
People of the Dead Sea Scrolls: Essenes or Sadducees?	James C. Vanderkam	Bible Review	April 1991
Rule of Saint Benedict in English, The	St. Benedict; edited by Timothy Fry, O.S.B.	The Liturgical Press	1982
Smalcald Articles: Articles of Christian Doctrine, The	Dr. Martin Luther, 1537; Translated by F. Bente And W. H. T. Dau	Ages Software	1999
Works of Josephus, The	Translated by William Whiston (1736)	Ages Software	1998
Works of Martin Luther, Vol. 4, The	Martin Luther	Ages Software	1998
World Book Encyclopedia		Field Enterprises Educational Corporation	1963
Your Book of Abbeys	David Jones	Faber & Faber	1979

Web sites referenced:

http://www.ocso.org/HTM/net/faq-eng.htm
http://www.jesuit.org/index.php/main/about-us/faqs/
http://www.newadvent.org/cathen/02784b.htm
http://poorclare.org/
http://www.brigittine.org/monks/ab0711.html
http://www.newadvent.org/cathen/14515b.htm
http://www.newadvent.org/cathen/11001a.htm

The Author on YouTube

There are a number of lectures on Christian historical and theological topics on YouTube by the author, including:

- An Introduction to the Apocrypha and the Septuagint
- Albigensian Crusade and the Start of the Papal Inquisition, The
- Comparing Essenes and Christian Monks
- Dead Sea Scrolls Timeline
- Did Christ Appear in the Old Testament as Melchizedek?
- Discovery of the Dead Sea Scrolls
- Discovery of the Grave of King Arthur
- Does the pre-incarnate Christ appear in the Old Testament?
- First Crusade, The
- History of Protestantism in the US: 1900-1950 Timeline
- History of Protestantism in the US: 1950-2000 Timeline
- Impact of the Scopes Monkey Trial on Protestantism
- King Arthur and Glastonbury
- Maccabean Revolt
- Named Angels: Gabriel, Michael
- Origins of the New Testament: Athanasius
- Rise of Pentecostalism
- Significance and impact of the Crusades
- Significance of Martin Luther
- Tobit (from the course "The Apocrypha and Christianity")

To find these lectures, search on "jone442" in YouTube.

About the Author

Robert C. Jones grew up in the Philadelphia, Pennsylvania area. In 1981, he moved to the Atlanta, Georgia area, where he received a B.S. in Computer Science at DeVry Institute of Technology. From 1984-2009, Robert worked for Hewlett-Packard as a computer consultant. He now works as an independent computer support and video services consultant.

Robert is an ordained elder in the Presbyterian Church. He has written and taught numerous adult Sunday School courses. He has also been active in choir ministries over the years, and has taught the Disciples Bible Study six times. He is the author of *A Brief History of Protestantism in the United States, A Brief History of the Sacraments: Baptism and Communion, Heaven and Hell: In the Bible, the Apocrypha and the Dead Sea Scrolls, The Crusades and the Inquisition: A Brief History, Monks and Monasteries: A Brief History,* and *Meet the Apostles: Biblical and Legendary Accounts*.

Robert is President of the Kennesaw Historical Society, for whom he has written several books, including *The Law Heard 'Round the World - An Examination of the Kennesaw Gun Law and Its Effects on the Community, Retracing the Route of the General - Following in the Footsteps of the Andrews Raid,* and *Images of America: Kennesaw*.

Robert has also written several books on ghost towns in the Southwest, including in Death Valley, Nevada, Arizona, New Mexico, and Mojave National Preserve.

In 2005, Robert co-authored a business-oriented book entitled *Working Virtually: The Challenges of Virtual Teams*.

His interests include the Civil War, Medieval Monasteries, American railroads, ghost towns, hiking in Death Valley and the Mojave, and Biblical Archaeology.

robertcjones@mindspring.com

Cover: Trappist Monastery of the Holy Spirit in Conyers, Georgia (Photo by Robert C. Jones)

8827885R00063

Printed in Great Britain
by Amazon.co.uk, Ltd.,
Marston Gate.